TAKE ACTION!

LESSON PLANS FOR THE MULTICULTURAL CLASSROOM

Lori Langer de Ramírez
Herricks Public SchoolsNew Hyde Park, NY

Merrill
is an imprint of

Upper Saddle River, New Jersey
Columbus, Ohio

Library of Congress Cataloging-in-Publication Data

Langer de Ramirez, Lori.
    Take action! : lesson plans for the multicultural classroom / Lori
Langer de Ramirez.
        p. cm.
    Includes index.
    ISBN-13: 978-0-13-157350-5
    ISBN-10: 0-13-157350-0
    1. Multicultural education—United States—Curricula—Planning
I. Title.
    LC1099. 3 . L363 2009
    371.117—dc22   2007039959

Vice President and Executive Publisher: Jeffery W. Johnston
Executive Editor: Darcy Betts Prybella
Editorial Assistant: Nancy J. Holstein
Project Manager: Sarah N. Kenoyer
Production Coordinator: Christian Holdener, S4Carlisle Publishing Services
Copy Editor: Robert L. Marcum
Design Coordinator: Diane C. Loerenzo
Text Design and Illustrations: S4Carlisle Publishing Services
Cover Design: Jason Moore
Cover Image: Jupiter Images
Operations Specialist: Susan W. Hannahs
Director of Marketing: Quinn Perkson
Marketing Coordinator: Brian Mounts

This book was set in Garamond by S4Carlisle Publishing Services. It was printed and bound by R. R. Donnelley & Sons Company. The cover was printed by Phoenix Color Corp.

Photo Credits: Joanna Keenan, p. 15; Lori Langer de Ramirez, p. 36, 54, 62, 85, 104, 127, 153, 168; Doug Anderson, p. 91

Pearson Education Ltd.
Pearson Education Singapore Pte. Ltd.
Pearson Education Canada, Ltd.
Pearson Education–Japan

Pearson Education Australia Pty. Limited
Pearson Education North Asia Ltd.
Pearson Educación de Mexico, S.A. de C.V.
Pearson Education Malaysia Pte. Ltd.

Merrill
is an imprint of

10 9 8 7 6 5 4 3 2 1
ISBN-13: 978-0-13-157350-5
ISBN-10:   0-13-157350-0

I dedicate this book to my husband, Ramón Ramírez, whose keen insights about human nature, whose generosity of spirit, and whose unconditional love inspire and elevate me . . . every day.

■ PREFACE

THE THEORY BEHIND THE BOOK

In my years teaching a graduate course at Teachers College, Columbia University entitled "Teaching and Learning in the Multicultural Classroom," many lesson plan ideas were shared. The course served as a forum for the discussion of issues surrounding multicultural education and diversity. In working with teachers in this course—and in my own experience as a teacher and teacher educator—I have found that we teachers learn best from each other in small groups and in informal discussions about our practice. Furthermore, we all benefit from sharing practical ideas and suggestions. For this reason, as a final project, I required students to develop a lesson in which they address some issue of diversity. The lesson and unit plans that were generated as a result of this assignment were one of the highlights of the course. Students expressed a great deal of appreciation for these very practical suggestions about how to meet the needs of diverse learners in our classrooms.

The concept of this book—lessons leading to an action project—is grounded firmly in Paulo Freire's notion of *conscientização*. This Portuguese term "refers to learning to perceive social, political, and economic contradictions, and to take action against the oppressive elements of reality" (Myra Bergman Ramos, translator's note, p. 35). In his important work, *Pedagogy of the Oppressed* (New York: Continuum, 2000), Freire urged educators to form a praxis, a combination of reflection, dialogue, and action. It is on this melding of thought, theory, and dialog with activity and action that this book is designed.

The book also strives to situate issues of diversity and multiculturalism within the paradigm of power struggles, issues of hegemony, and the idea of oppressive force outlined in Freire's works. Thus Freire's concepts not only help to structure the format of the book (i.e., praxis = a combination of theory, dialog, and activity), but also provide a lens through which to view the current theory on the many topics surrounding multicultural education.

THE STRUCTURE OF THE BOOK

Each lesson contains a step-by-step activity guide that leads to an action project for students. The action project serves as both a culminating activity and a prompt for further investigation. It is meant to provide some closure for the lesson, but also to give students and teachers a jumping-off point for deeper and more sustained work on the topic. The project might involve students in educating others in the school community, creating resources, or establishing new programs. It might involve writing letters of protest or support for an important issue, or have students doing service projects in the community. Overall, the action project is meant to get teachers and students to take action and make positive change in their community.

HOW TO USE THIS BOOK

Each chapter begins with a quote, proverb, or saying that relates to the chapter topic. Teachers might use this quote as a means of sparking conversation with students or as a writing prompt for reflective journal entries.

Some Background

The quote is followed by a brief introduction to the chapter topic. This introduction includes some theory and important issues to consider when diving into the lessons to follow.

Lesson Preparation for the Teacher

This section includes three subsections that you, the teacher, can explore prior to working on any of the lessons that follow.

The first part begins with a narrative entitled **One Teacher's Reflection.** These are stories written by teachers who reflect on specific incidents related to the chapter topic. These stories come from their own classroom and are meant to stimulate your thinking about the connection between theory and practice.

Following the narrative, you will find a **Teacher Action Project.** As with the action projects designed for students, these teacher action projects are meant to inspire deeper, more global connections between you and the chapter topic. You might be prompted to visit other classrooms, other schools, or other communities. The projects are meant to expose you to the chapter topics in a more visceral way than if the preparation had only been through reading.

Under the final subheading, **References and Suggested Reading,** you will find further reading materials and references. The information is meant to extend the action projects by providing you with more tools for developing further lessons and projects for your own students.

Lesson Plans for the Multicultural Classroom

Following the teacher preparation section, the lessons are divided among three categories, Elementary (K–5), Middle School (6–8), and High School (9–12) lessons with one example of each level provided for each topic/chapter. The lessons are prefaced by a brief section of background information related to the specific lesson topic. This information is provided primarily for you, the teacher, but can often be used as part of the lesson as a means of providing background information for students as well.

Take Action! DVD

Explore this unique DVD, packaged with the text, to observe video of teachers at various grade levels (elementary, middle, and high school) using nine of the multicultural lesson plans found in this text. See detailed descriptions of each video lesson following the Table of Contents.

Predictable Lesson Plan Format

All lesson plans in the collection follow a standard "recipe" format and can be easily reproduced or modified as needed.

- **Heading:** Provides a title for the lesson.
- **Grade Levels:** A general grade range for which the lesson is most appropriate. Note that despite the suggestion of grade levels, every school context is different. What works in a sixth grade classroom in a small rural school district in Iowa, might not work as well in a large urban district such as Los Angeles or New York. Each teacher will have to determine if the grade recommendation is right for their students. If it isn't, you should feel comfortable adapting the lessons to work in your own school context.
- **Content Areas Addressed:** A list of subject or content areas that are touched upon in the lesson and/or action project.
- **Topic:** A brief description of the main topic or topics to be addressed in the lesson.
- **Rationale for Using This Lesson:** This section seeks to answer the "why bother?" question when deciding what curriculum to include in one's class. It provides a sense of the importance of the topic of the lesson.
- **Background Information:** Provides you and your students with some necessary information about the main topic(s) in the lesson.
- **Goals/Aims:** Gives a sense for what you can expect students to be able to accomplish or do during the lesson and/or as a result of the action project.
- **Connections to Standards:** Links to national standards for all the content areas that are included in the lesson. While many states have particular state standards, in this book we use national standards for greater applicability across the United States.

You may easily correlate the national standards listed in the book to your own state standards by connecting to your individual state education websites. The national standards used in the book were culled from national professional organizations specific to each subject area as well as the excellent compendium of content standards and benchmarks for K–12 education located on the McREL (Mid-continent Research for Education and Learning) website (http//:www.mcrel.org). They are reprinted at each lesson by the kind permission of McREL.

- **Materials:** A "recipe-style" list of the materials needed to do all of the activities in the lesson and action project.
- **Activity:** A step-by-step description of the tasks or activities in the lesson.
- **Action Project:** A task that helps translate the topic of the lesson into a project that helps benefit the class, the school, or the community.
- **Reflection:** Questions to reflect on after having presented the lesson to students. These questions may serve as prompts for discussion with colleagues or as topics for reflective journal entries.
- **Resource Page (as applicable):** Photocopiable handout pages that are connected to the lesson.

It is the aim of this book to provide you as a teacher with ways to incorporate multicultural teaching into your classroom and school. The lessons should start conversations, forge connections to different topics of identity and diversity, and inspire further research. The culminating projects are meant to prompt students and teachers alike to take action and do something to balance inequities, fight discrimination, and help to change the world—one step at a time.

Reference

Freire, P. (2000). *Pedagogy of the oppressed*. New York: Continuum.

ACKNOWLEDGEMENTS

For more than 20 semesters of teaching my course, "Teaching and Learning in the Multicultural Classroom" at Teachers College, Columbia University, I asked my students to design and develop their own multicultural lesson plans. The quality and creativity that resulted both amazed and inspired me. The book you are now holding contains several of the best of these lesson plans, along with others written by colleagues and experts and educators from around the United States. I would like to thank the following people for their lesson plans and/or text and photographic contributions to this book: Doug Anderson, Maya Ban, Jill Baron, Paula Davis, Frank DeCelie, H. Edward Deluzain, Cara Fenner, David B. Givens, Paul Gorski, David W. Gurney, Shelley Greenspan Dreizen, Judie Haynes, Nick Ip, Victor Jaccarino, Alix Morgan, Pablo Muirhead, Michael Orlep, Yelena Patish, Melissa Pesce, Edmund Sass, Sarah Senter, Peter Tatchell, and Jodi Thompson. I would also like to thank the following people for their reviews: Theresa Garfield, Palo Alto College; Emiliano Gonzalez, University of St. Thomas; Kim Hackford-Peer, University of Utah; Nancy L. Hadaway, University of Texas at Arlington; Linda Nowell, California State University-Sacramento; Angela L. Pedrana, University of Houston-Downtown; Patricia M. Ryan, Otterbein College; Yer Thao, Portland State University; Joy L. Wiggins, University of Texas at Arlington.

I would also like to thank Debbie Stollenwerk for envisioning the DVD portion of this project and for always being an enthusiastic supporter of my work. Thanks to Darcy Betts and Amy Nelson for being patient with all my questions and helpful in so many ways, and to Carl Harris for his excellent filming of the DVD lessons. Thanks to Christian Holdener at S4Carlisle Publishing Services for shepherding the project to completion. And a very special thanks to my extraordinarily talented copyeditor, Robert L. Marcum, for pushing me to answer the "tough questions" and for polishing the manuscript until it sparkles.

■ BRIEF CONTENTS

CONTENTS

Note: Every effort has been made to provide accurate and current Internet information in this book. However, the Internet and information posted on it are constantly changing, so it is inevitable that some of the Internet addresses listed in this textbook will change.

■ CONTENTS FOR TAKE ACTION! DVD

The Universal Declaration of Human Rights (Lesson 3)

High School, Social Studies

In this video clip, a high school Social Studies class, focusing on model United Nations, discusses the Universal Declaration of Human Rights. The class first discusses the nature of human rights, then students break into groups to make posters that report human rights violations around the world. Students make important connections to a variety of issues that often reflect their home cultures and religious beliefs. They also engage in interdisciplinary learning by connecting to a variety of subject areas in this lesson. As you watch the video, notice how students bring their home cultures into the discussions.
Running Time: 13:31, Page 15

Schools and Freedom of Expression (Lesson 6)

High School, Social Studies

In this video clip, a high school Social Studies class brainstorms ways that people visually express identity. The teacher provides students with an assortment of current court cases involving students and dress. Students work in groups to connect their understandings of constitutional law with their own cultural backgrounds and beliefs to come up with rulings on the cases. As you watch the video, notice how the teacher makes consistent reference throughout the lesson to her students and their experiences relating to the issue of dress and expression of identity in school.
Running Time: 13:56, Page 36

The 14th Amendment of Our Schools (Lesson 9)

High School (10th grade), Social Studies

In this video clip, high school Social Studies students read, discuss, and debate two court cases dealing with 14th amendment issues. After reading the cases, students divide into two large groups, one for each case, that take responsibility for understanding the case and presenting the details to the rest of the class. Students learn about issues affecting immigrant groups by relating issues like tuition, taxes, and quality of education to their own contexts. As you watch the video, notice how the teacher breaks down complicated issues into concepts that these sophomore students can both understand and relate to their own lives.
Running Time: 18:32, Page 54

FDR's Secret (Lesson 10)

Elementary

In this video clip, elementary school students brainstorm reasons someone might hide a disability then explore the life and presidency of Franklin Delano Roosevelt, focusing on the question: "Was FDR successful at hiding his disability?" The teacher attends to students with different learning styles by providing photographs and historical cartoons of FDR and then asks small groups to come to their own answer to the question. As you watch the video, notice how the teacher connects a general discussion of disabilities to a specific case such as FDR's as a means of providing students with the opportunity to discuss this issue.
Running Time: 11:15, Page 62

Geometry and Tessellation in Islamic Art (Lesson 14)

Middle School, Computers

In this video clip, middle school students view examples of architectural sites in India as the teacher points out instances of geometric patterns and tessellations in the images. The teacher explains how these shapes carry important religious significance in Islamic art. After a computer demonstration, students are allowed to create their own computer images using a drawing program. As you watch the video, notice how the teacher expands the lesson and connects to the real-world by encouraging students to explore beyond the classroom.
Running Time: 14:22, Page 85

We Are All in the Dumps with Jack and Guy (Lesson 16)

Elementary

In this video clip, elementary school students begin by brainstorming the word "home" then read a Maurice Sendak picture book about homelessness, poverty, and other sensitive issues. Following the reading, students meet in groups to write and illustrate a nursery rhyme about homelessness that mimics the rhyme structure of the book they just read. As you watch the video, notice how the teacher connects the topic in the story to the lives of the students in his class. Running Time: 13:26, Page 104

Talking With Your Body (Lesson 19)

Elementary (2nd grade)

In this video clip, a class of second grade students discusses non-verbal communication (gestures and facial expressions) and explores its meanings across cultures. Students are asked to predict if particular gestures are rude or not and then create their own greeting gestures. As you watch the video, notice how the teacher handles students' responses to the gesture assignment, especially one student who unwittingly demonstrates a rude gesture for the class. Running Time: 13:32, Page 127

Rosalind Franklin—The Other Discover of DNA (Lesson 23)

Middle School (6th grade), Gifted and Talented Physical Science

In this video clip, a class of sixth grade students learns about scientist Rosalind Franklin, who was not originally credited for her important contributions to the discovery of DNA. As students are told about Dr. Franklin's work, they assume that the teacher is talking about a male scientist. When it is revealed that Dr. Watson was a woman, students are surprised and then discuss their reactions. As you watch the video, notice how the teacher sets up the discussion so that students make their own assumptions about the gender of Rosalind Franklin. Notice also how the teacher leads the subsequent discussion about the lack of credit that Dr. Franklin received in her lifetime. Running Time: 19:59, Page 153

Am I Blue? (Lesson 26)

Middle School (8th grade), English Language Arts

In this video clip, eighth grade English Language Arts students read a short story entitled "Am I Blue?" that deals with issues such as homophobia, gay bashing, and sexual identity. Students discuss the events in the book while unpacking the meaning of terms like "gay" and "homophobic" and comments such as "that's so gay." As you watch the video, notice how the teacher incorporates students' experiences and current events into the discussion in order to connect the story to the students' lives. Running Time: 21:11, Page 168

CHAPTER 1

DOING MULTICULTURAL EDUCATION

I want American history taught.
Unless I'm in that book, you're not in it either.

JAMES BALDWIN (U.S. writer, 1924–1987)

Some Background

As teachers, we are under so much pressure to include a variety of topics, themes, and skills in our curricula. Whether we teach kindergarten or middle school math, there seems to be a never-ending list of new strategies to try, standards to address, or benchmarks to meet. It can be frustrating when we attempt to "make it all fit" into our limited school day. For this reason—and for many others—the idea of "doing" multicultural education can seem overwhelming at best, and unfeasible at worst.

Many educators view multicultural education as something to be added to the curriculum. It might take the form of adding new titles to a high school literature class or adding a cultural celebration to a particular month. When multicultural education is viewed in additive terms (to use James Banks's term), it is no wonder that it can be viewed as an imposition. Because it is most often wedged into an already hectic educational schedule, it is logical that teachers regard it as suspect, as an imposition, or as something to be "done" in a one-time celebration or festival.

But multicultural education need not impose on a curriculum. If treated as something to be integrated rather than added, multiculturalism becomes a seamless part of a diversity-rich curriculum. Rather than steal time from the important skills to be mastered for standardized tests, it evolves into the support, grid, or structure on which all lessons—from algebra to zoology—can be supported.

So what IS multicultural education? Figure 1.1 presents a useful chart of the *IS* and the *ISN'T* of multicultural education:

Another way of looking at multicultural education is through the lens of approaches outlined by James Banks (2003):

> **The Contributions Approach.** In this approach, teachers might make reference to a culture's most popular heroes, holidays, foods, or costumes. This approach often involves special festivals, performances, or celebrations.

Figure 1.1 The IS and ISN'T of multicultural education.

Multicultural Education *ISN'T*	Multicultural Education *IS*
1. about everyone agreeing and getting along	1. about naming and eliminating the inequities in education
2. only applicable to Language Arts and History	2. a comprehensive approach for making education more inclusive, active, and engaging in all subject areas
3. a process of watering down good curriculum	3. a process for presenting all students with a more comprehensive, accurate understanding of the world
4. related only to curriculum reform	4. related to all aspects of education including pedagogy, counseling, administration, assessment and evaluation, research, etc.
5. only for teachers and students of color	5. for *ALL* students and educators
6. achieved through a series of small changes	6. achieved through the reexamination and transformation of all aspects of education
7. modeled through cultural bulletin boards, assemblies, or fairs	7. modeled through self-critique, self-examination, and cross-cultural relationship-building
8. the responsibility of culture-based student clubs or organizations	8. the responsibility of teachers, administrators, and school staff
9. a single in-service workshop	9. an on-going commitment

Source: Copyright © 2007 Paul C. Gorski, http://www.edchange.org. Reprinted by permission.

The Additive Approach. In this approach, literature, concepts, or themes might be added to the curriculum. The curriculum as such is not changed, only broadened to include more information.

The Transformation Approach. Here the structure of the curriculum is changed to allow students to view concepts (e.g., in history or literature) from a variety of viewpoints.

The Social Action Approach. While studying a topic, students are encouraged to give opinions, make decisions, and take action on a subject. Students take an active role in the curriculum.

These approaches can be seen as a continuum, with the contributions approach being the easiest to implement, yet also the most superficial way of "doing" multiculturalism in schools. Both the transformation and social action approaches are more challenging to implement, but they allow students access to multiple viewpoints and inspire them to take action and change their world for the better.

As you read through this book and start using the lessons with your students, think of ways to incorporate multicultural education into your teaching on a sustained level. While the lessons in this book are almost all stand-alone snapshots of good multicultural teaching, the real key to integrating multiculturalism into your classroom comes from you, the teacher. Begin with one lesson and keep weaving more activities, units, projects, and topics into your curriculum until there is no such thing as a "multicultural lesson," but rather just a "really great teaching opportunity."

Lesson Preparation for the Teacher

ONE TEACHER'S REFLECTION: OUR SCHOOL'S TOWER OF BABEL

There are over 40 languages spoken by students in our schools. This seems incredible to me. Some of these students are English Language Learners. Others are not. Some are literate in their home languages. Others are not. Some are proud to be multilingual. Others are not. I wanted to do something to tap into this wonderful resource, so I instituted a "Students-as-Teachers" language program.

During the month of February, I sent out "job applications" looking for student language teachers. Students were asked what language they could teach, how they would teach it to their fellow students in a 30-minute class, and why they wanted to teach it. All month their applications flowed into my office:

> *Tamil, Fukinese, Norwegian, and Greek*
>
> *Mandarin Chinese, Korean, Malayalam, and Hebrew*

Some students wanted to teach the alphabet and some basic greetings. Others planned to include cultural elements such as food and music. Almost all reported that they wanted to share their identities with their classmates.

By March there were 30 classes scheduled. Teachers, administrators, and students attended these after-school classes in droves. We learned to dance Navratri dances, write Chinese characters, and greet each other in Polish. The participants reported feeling "impressed" and "amazed" by how beautiful, complicated, and interesting the languages were. The student/teachers felt incredible pride in being able to share their identities in the school context.

This was only a month-long event, only one attempt to tap into the wealth of information and experience that our multilingual/multicultural students bring into our schools. I can't help but feel like a fraud, though. Is this really enough? What happens after that month of March? How can we extend the experience and integrate it more into the school day? Are we simply adding a one-off event as a means of acknowledging difference rather than weaving it into the curriculum? If this activity isn't enough, then what is?

TEACHER ACTION PROJECT: COMPARING MULTICULTURALISMS

Just as there is a variety of schools in the United States, there are many ways to "do" multicultural education. Explore two schools' ways of including diversity in the curriculum. Choose two schools in your own district, neighborhood, or town. Arrange for a visit to each school with a school official. Many schools have multicultural festivals, celebrations, or other stand-alone events. Others will have multicultural themes woven throughout the curriculum. Try to find two schools that represent these two different ends of the multicultural continuum. (Note: If you are unable to make an actual visit to a school or classroom, take a virtual visit on the Web. Search online for two schools that provide information about their multicultural education programs, events, or curricula.)

During the visit, try to attain answers to these WH–questions:

1. **Who** participates in the multicultural events/curriculum?

2. **Who** determines what topics will be addressed/included? (Note: you may need to interview faculty, staff, and/or students to answer this question.)

3. **What** does the multicultural program look like? (i.e., a celebration? A public event? An exploration? A sustained effort?)

4. **Where** does the multicultural event take place? (i.e., the auditorium? The cafeteria? The library? The classroom?)

5. **When** is multiculturalism and diversity addressed? (i.e., one week during the year? One month? All the time?)

6. **Why** are the programs/events celebrated the way they are? (i.e., what are the goals/aims of the programs or events?) (Note: you may need to interview faculty, staff, and/or students to answer this question.)

Using information from your observations and answers to the questions, write a case study report about each school's multicultural efforts. Based on Banks's approaches to multicultural education, label each of the two schools. Which school seems to be closer to the transformation approach that Banks describes? How might the other school move closer to this approach?

If you feel comfortable with the faculty in any of the schools you visited, share your report with a colleague, a supervisor, or the principal of that school. Discuss whether your report reflects the school's own image of its multicultural curriculum.

References and Suggested Readings

Banks, J. A. (2007). *An introduction to multicultural education* (4th ed.). Boston: Allyn & Bacon.

Banks, J. A., & McGee Banks, C. A. (2003). *Handbook of research in multicultural education.* San Francisco, CA: Jossey-Bass.

Banks, J. A., & McGee Banks, C. A. (2006). *Multicultural education: Issues and perspectives* (6th ed.). New York: Wiley.

Bigelow, B., Christensen, L., Karp, S., Miner, B., & Peterson, B. (Eds.). (1994). *Rethinking our classrooms: Teaching for equity and justice.* Montgomery, AL: Rethinking Schools, Ltd.

Brown, S. C., & Kysilka, M. L. (2002). *Applying multicultural and global concepts in the classroom and beyond.* Boston: Allyn & Bacon.

Davidman, L., & Davidman, P. (1997). *Teaching with a multicultural perspective: A practical guide.* White Plains, NY: Longman.

Dresser, N. (1996). *Multicultural manners: New rules of etiquette for a changing society.* Hoboken, New Jersey: Wiley.

Gollnick, D. M., & Chinn, P. C. (2005.) *Multicultural education in a pluralistic society & Exploring diversity package* (7th ed.). Upper Saddle River, NJ: Prentice Hall.

Grant, C., & Lei, J. (2001). *Global constructions of multicultural education: Theories and realities.* Mahwah, NJ: Lawrence Erlbaum Associates.

Grant, C. A., & Sleeter, C. E. (2003). *Turning on learning: Five approaches for multicultural teaching plans for race, class, gender and disability.* New York: Wiley.

Koppelman, K. L., & Goodhart, R. L. (2005). *Understanding human differences: Multicultural education for a diverse America.* New York: Pearson.

Lee, E., Menkart, D., & Okazawa-Rey, M. (Eds.). (1998). *Beyond heroes and holidays: A practical guide to k–12 anti-racist, multicultural education and staff development.* Washington, DC: Teaching for Change.

Lisi, P., & Rios, F. (Eds.). (2005). *Multicultural perspectives: The official journal of the National Association for Multicultural Education* (Vol. 7). Mahwah, NJ: Lawrence Erlbaum Associates.

Nieto, S. (1999). *The light in their eyes: Creating multicultural learning communities.* New York: Teachers College Press.

Reissman, R. (1994). *The evolving multicultural classroom.* Alexandria, VA: Association for Supervision and Curriculum Development.

Shulman, J., & Mesa-Bains, A. (1993). *Diversity in the classroom: A casebook for teachers and teacher educators.* Mahwah, NJ: Lawrence Erlbaum Associates.

Sleeter, C. E., & Grant, C. A. (2003). *Making choices for multicultural education: Five approaches to race, class, and gender.* New York: Wiley.

Takaki, R. (1993). *A different mirror: A history of multicultural America.* New York: Little, Brown.

Tiedt, P. L., & Tiedt, I. M. (2002). *Multicultural teaching: A handbook of activities, information, and resources.* Boston: Allyn & Bacon.

LESSON 1

CINDERELLA AROUND THE WORLD

GRADE LEVELS

Grades 1–5

CONTENT AREAS ADDRESSED

Geography, Language Arts, Life Skills, Theater

TOPIC

There are many versions of the "Cinderella story" from cultures all around the world. However, North American elementary students are probably most familiar with the animated Walt Disney version, *Cinderella* (1950). (The original version of Cinderella is commonly attributed to Charles Perrault, whose story was published in 1697 in Paris.) The fact that most children have not been exposed to the other cultural versions of the classic fairy tale presents a wonderful opportunity. Cinderella stories can be used to explore different cultures and improve multicultural awareness.

RATIONALE FOR USING THIS LESSON

By comparing and contrasting different versions of this familiar story, students can come to a greater understanding of the ways in which culture affects the belief systems, morals, and ethics of a people. While details, setting, and characters are culture specific, many themes will be found to be universal. Students will also be able to make connections to story traditions in their own cultural backgrounds.

BACKGROUND INFORMATION: THE HISTORY OF CINDERELLA

Fairy tale. It is distinguished from other varieties of folktale by its world of "wish fulfillment" (Rohrich 1988, 8). Germany's Grimm brothers, Jacob and Wilhelm, were not composers of fairy and folktales, but instead "retold and rewrote what they had remembered from childhood or obtained through questioning" (Degh 1988, 69). Though nineteenth century scholars praised the brothers for preserving oral tales, modern scholars often criticize the Grimms for mixing oral and literary traditions and for possibly corrupting the tales of the "folk" by adding their own style and embellishments (69–70). Whether or not one appreciates the work of the brothers, no one can deny their significance. The *Household Tales* is the most frequently translated and reprinted German book next to the Bible (76).

"Cinderella" is among the *Household Tales*, of which the earliest publication date is 1812. Her character was somewhat altered between this version and those later printings. According to scholar Ruth B. Bottigheimer, the earlier Cinderella is bold enough to volunteer herself to try on the slipper because Wilhelm's earlier version was heavily influenced by the bourgeoisie; but the "common folk" who influenced the later versions believed in a harsher life for women in which they should be silent (1988, 198). Hence, the later Cinderella does not try on the shoe until the prince insists.

The earliest known European version of the tale dates back to 1634, but *Yeh-Shen*, the Chinese Cinderella story, precedes any European version by several centuries. It was first recorded in a book called *The Miscellaneous Record of Yu Yang* from the T'ang dynasty of 618–907 A.D. (Louie, 1982).

Even older, still, is the Egyptian Cinderella story, *The Girl with the Rose-Red Slippers*. This is the earliest known version of the story, dating all the way back to 570–526 B.C. (Green 1956; pp. 221).

(From Senter, S. (2007). *Cinderella history*. Retrieved June 11, 2007 from http://web.utk.edu/~ssenter/fairytale2.html)

References

Bottigheimer, R. B. (1988). From gold to guilt: The forces which reshaped *Grimms' tales*. In McGlathery, J. M., Danielson, L. W., Lorbe, R. E., & Richardson, S. K. (Eds.), *The brothers Grimm and folktale* (pp. 192–204). Chicago: University of Illinois Press.

Degh, L. (1988). What did the Grimm brothers give to and take from the folk? In McGlathery, J. M., Danielson, L. W., Lorbe, R. E., & Richardson, S. K. (Eds.), *The brothers Grimm and folktale* (pp. 66–90). Chicago: University of Illinois Press.

Green, R. L. (1956). The girl with the rose-red slippers. In Roger Lancelyn Green, *Tales of ancient Egypt* (pp. 213–214). London: Penguin.

Louie, A. (1982). *Yeh-Shen—A Cinderella story from China*. New York: Philomel.

Rohrich, L. (1988). The quest of meaning in folk narrative research. In McGlathery, J. M., Danielson, L. W., Lorbe, R. E., & Richardson, S. K. (Eds.), *The brothers Grimm and folktale* (pp. 1–15). Chicago: University of Illinois Press.

GOALS/AIMS

- Students will be able to recognize the main components of a story (e.g., plot, setting, theme, characterization, etc.).
- Students will be able to communicate their questions about and reactions to literature.
- Students will be able to compare stories on a common theme that derive from different cultures and pinpoint their similarities and differences.
- Students will be able to strengthen their writing and storytelling abilities as they develop an adaptation of other well-known stories.
- Students will be able to learn about different cultures and improve multicultural awareness.

CONNECTIONS TO STANDARDS

- *Geography Standard 1:* Uses maps and other geographic representations, tools, and technologies to acquire, process, and report information.
- *Language Arts Writing Standard 1:* Uses general skills and strategies of the writing process.
- *Life Skills—Working with others: Standard 1:* Contributes to the overall effort of a group.

- *Life Skills—Working with others: Standard 4:* Displays effective interpersonal communication skills.
- *Theater: Standard 1:* Demonstrates competence in writing scripts.
- *Theater: Standard 2:* Uses acting skills.
- *Theater: Standard 3:* Designs and produces informal and formal productions.

(Copyright 2007. Reprinted with permission from *Content Knowledge: A Compendium of Standards and Benchmarks for K-12 Education,* 4th ed. http://www.mcrel.org/standards-benchmarks/ All rights reserved.)

MATERIALS

- Lesson 1 Resource Page: Story Map Chart
- World map
- Different colored pushpins
- A variety of Cinderella stories from various cultures, such as the following:
    - *Cinderella* by C. Perrault, L. Koopmans, and Loek Koopmans
    - *Walt Disney's Cinderella* retold by Cynthia Rylant
    - *Cendrillon: A Caribbean Cinderella* by Robert D. San Souci
    - *Fair, Brown and Trembling: An Irish Cinderella Story* by Jude Daly
    - *Domitila: A Cinderella Tale from the Mexican Tradition* by Jewell Reinhart Coburn
    - *The Golden Sandal: A Middle Eastern Cinderella Story* by Rebecca Hickox
    - *The Gift of the Crocodile: A Cinderella Story* by Judy Sierra
    - *Smoky Mountain Rose: An Appalachian Cinderella* by Alan Schroeder
    - *Yeh-Shen: A Cinderella Story from China* by Ai-Ling Louie
    - *Mufaro's Beautiful Daughters: An African Tale* by John Steptoe
    - *The Korean Cinderella* by Shirley Climo
    - *The Egyptian Cinderella* by Shirley Climo
    - *Sootface: An Ojibwa Cinderella Story* by Robert San Souci

For more titles, refer to the *Sur La Lune Fairytales* website (http://www.surlalunefairytales.com).

ACTIVITY

1. Begin by reading the widely known Disney/Perrault version of the Cinderella story.
2. Discuss each story using comprehension questions, such as these from the Egyptian Cinderella:
    - How is the dress of Rhodopis (the Egyptian Cinderella) different from the Cinderella you have previously read about? Why do you think they dress differently? Can anyone tell us how the climate of Egypt compares with the climate of the United States? (The teacher may want to show the students Egypt and the United States on the globe and on a map, to integrate geography into the lesson.)
    - How are Kipa and the other two servant girls like Cinderella's stepsisters? Do they treat Rhodopis fairly? Tell why you think they do or don't.
    - Does this story have a happy ending? Compare the way this story ends with the ending of Cinderella.
3. After each story, have students create a chart that lists the main components of the story (setting, characters, problem, resolution, etc.; see Lesson 1 Resource Page for a template). With younger students, this can also be done as a class.
4. Begin introducing new versions of the Cinderella story to the class. As you do this, use a pushpin to identify the country/region of origin of the story on a map.
5. Choose two stories to compare and contrast. Using a chart like that shown in Figure 1.2, have students compare and contrast the two tales. Ask them to think about

Figure 1.2 Comparing Cinderellas

Perrault's Cinderella	Things in Common	The Egyptian Cinderella
glass slippers	a type of shoe	rose-colored slipper
fairy godmother	a magical helper	the god Horus
the ball	a celebration	a court party

the themes or elements that are the same in each story (those elements go in the middle column). Then have students provide the details that make each story different. Encourage students to think about how the storytellers of each culture made the central story of Cinderella "their own."

6. Have students write/illustrate their own version of the Cinderella story, adapting it to their own culture. Arrange for them to visit other classrooms in the school to read their stories to other students.

ACTION PROJECT

Have students write/direct/perform a class play with a version of the Cinderella story. In this class version, each student should contribute one element from her/his culture to be represented in some way in the story. This could include costume, food, some aspect of the setting, names of characters, props, or content of the story. Arrange for your "troupe" to visit other classrooms/schools to perform their play. Ask audience members to list all of the cultural elements that they can observe from the performance. Have your "actors" discuss the elements and the play with the audience after the show.

REFLECTION

How did students respond to the different versions of the Cinderella story? Did they have a favorite? If so, which one? Why do you think that the students responded the way they did to the various versions of the story? What kinds of cultural elements did they choose to include in their own versions? What elements were included in the play version that the class created as a whole? What elements of culture do the elements included in the original stories represent? For example, are they mainly visible elements (i.e., clothing, food) or do they also include morals, beliefs, of other representations or nonmaterial culture?

WEB RESOURCES FOR "CINDERELLA" STORIES

Sur La Lune Fairytales: http://www.surlalunefairytales.com/cinderella/other.html

D. L. Ashliman's Cinderella Page: http://www.pitt.edu/~dash/type0510a.html

The Cinderella Project: http://www.usm.edu/english/fairytales/cinderella/cinderella.html

Lesson 1 adpated from Shelley Greenspan Dreizen's, *Cinderella Around the World.*
Used with permission.

LESSON 1 RESOURCE PAGE:
STORY MAP CHART

Title	
Country of Origin	
Setting	
Main Character	
Supporting Characters	
Problem	
Magic Elements	
Resolution	
Moral / Lesson Learned	

LESSON 2

THE BREADTH AND DEPTH OF "MULTICULTURAL"

Grades 6–8

CONTENT AREAS ADDRESSED

Language Arts, Life Skills, Math, Technology, Visual Arts

TOPIC

The Depth and Breadth of "Multicultural" is designed to engage students in a process of defining "*culture*" and examining its complexity. Often "culture" becomes synonymous with "race" or "ethnicity." This activity reveals the limitations of such a conceptualization and challenges the assumptions educators often may make about what students identify as the important strands of the "cultural" in "multicultural."

RATIONALE FOR USING THIS LESSON

This activity provides an excellent opportunity for you to make a link between critical pedagogy and multicultural teaching practices. The various steps in the lesson bring out the diversity of cultural dimensions, especially within the room of students you are working with. It is important for students to define what is culturally relevant to them. The lesson can help to illustrate to students how they themselves can be seen as important multicultural education resources.

BACKGROUND INFORMATION: HIDALGO'S THREE LEVELS OF CULTURE

In this activity, students will be working with Nitza Hidalgo's "three levels of culture." In working through the activity, it is vital to validate the views of the students. If they prefer to define themselves at the Concrete or the Behavioral level, it is best to not challenge them directly about that. (This may happen with some younger participant groups.) This activity can make some participants feel vulnerable, and it is important not to intensify that insecurity to the point that they are no longer participating.

Hidalgo's three levels of culture:

1. *Concrete:* This is the most visible and tangible level of culture, and includes the most surface-level dimensions, such as clothes, music, food, games, and so on. These aspects of culture are often those that provide the focus for multicultural "festivals" or "celebrations."

2. *Behavioral:* This level of culture clarifies how we define our social roles, the language we speak, and our approaches to nonverbal communication. The Behavioral level

reflects our language, gender roles, family structure, political affiliation, and other items that situate us organizationally in society.

3. *Symbolic:* This level of culture includes our values and beliefs. It can be abstract, but it is most often the key to how individuals define themselves. It includes values systems, customs, spirituality, religion, worldview, beliefs, and mores.

(From Hidalgo, N. (1993). Multicultural teacher introspection. In T. Perry & J. Fraser (Eds.) *Freedom's Plow: Teaching in the Multicultural Classroom* (pp. 99–106). New York: Routledge)

GOALS/AIMS

- Students will be able to think concretely about different aspects of cultural identity.
- Students will be able to categorize different aspects of cultural identity by Hidalgo's three levels.
- Students will communicate their findings with each other and to the school community at large.

CONNECTIONS TO STANDARDS

- *Language Arts Writing Standard 1:* Uses general skills and strategies of the writing process.
- *Language Arts Writing Standard 4:* Gathers and uses information for research purposes.
- *Language Arts Listening and Speaking Standard 8:* Uses listening and speaking strategies for different purposes.
- *Life Skills Standard 4:* Displays effective interpersonal communication skills.
- *Mathematics Standard 6:* Understands and applies basic and advanced concepts of statistics and data analysis.
- *Mathematics Standard 8:* Understands and applies basic and advanced properties of functions and algebra (understands how graphs can represent patterns).
- *Technology Standard 6:* Understands the nature and uses of different forms of technology.
- *Visual Arts Standard 1:* Understands and applies media, techniques, and processes related to the visual arts.
- *Visual Arts Standard 4:* Understands the visual arts in relation to history and cultures.

(Copyright 2007. Reprinted with permission from *Content Knowledge: A Compendium of Standards and Benchmarks for K-12 Education*, 4th ed. http://www.mcrel.org/standards-benchmarks/ All rights reserved.)

MATERIALS

- Chalkboard or large sheet of paper. At the top center, write "MULTICULTURAL."
- Poster paper
- Magazines for cutting out pictures/images
- Scissors
- Computer with graphing program such as Microsoft *Excel* (Note: If there is no access to computers, students can create the pie chart using a protractor and ruler)

1. *Defining* "multicultural". Start by underlining the prefix "*multi*" and asking your students what this prefix means. Responses will include "many," "varied or various," "different," and so on. Affirm all answers, then sum them up. This portion should only take a couple of minutes.

2. Next, move on to "*-cultural.*" What does this term mean? Encourage students to define "*cultural*" both in terms of what they believe a dictionary-type definition to be and what it means to them individually.

3. Tell the students you would like them to explore the understanding of "cultural" more deeply. Ask them to suggest all dimensions of culture they can think of, encouraging them to reflect on their own culture and the dimensions of that culture with which they identify. There are several effective ways of accomplishing this task. You can either have students call out these aspects of culture when they think of them (perhaps even using a student volunteer to list them under the heading on the board or chart). You might also decide to simply go around the room, person by person, asking for suggestions. There are literally endless dimensions to culture, and this will be reflected in the answers. It is likely that an influx of answers will come right away, then the rate of response will slow down considerably. This often happens after some of the more surface-level cultural aspects are suggested: music, food, and so on. Encourage the students to think a little more deeply about how they define their culture. Allow for some short silences, or suggest some deeper dimensions, including faith, religion, values, language, family structure, and others. It will be important to get as many suggestions for this list as possible. Also, point out how intertwined some of the dimensions are, illustrating how simplistic it is to make a judgment about somebody based on one cultural dimension of the person. This step should take 10 to 15 minutes.

4. *What's not there?* Several interesting cultural dimensions are likely to be ignored by students. Ironically, these are the very dimensions that are most often associated with multicultural education: race, gender, sexual orientation, social class. Do not suggest these additions to the list, because if nobody suggests them, the absence of these terms often leads to a fruitful conversation. If your class does not suggest one or more of these items, point this out and ask why the participants believe they didn't think of these dimensions. This will be an interesting introduction to the following steps. It's often the case that when participants are suggesting items for the list from their own experience—and thus through how they define themselves—race, gender, and so on don't come directly to their minds. But, if they're suggesting items for the list based on how others define them, or how they define OTHERS, these items immediately come to mind.

5. *Categorizing list items.* Divide the items into categories, which will make the final step of the exercise much easier. Indicate this intention to the group, and mention that you will be using Nitza Hidalgo's (1993) "three levels of culture" (see Background Information).

6. Write short definitions for these levels on the board or sheet of paper you used to record the dimensions of culture. Review each of the categories for a couple of minutes. Give the participants an opportunity to consider further how they define themselves within these categories. Ask them to look over the categories and the items on the board for a few seconds. As a group, categorize all items into these categories. There may be some disagreement about where a certain item falls, so allow the same item to be listed under two categories.

7. *Consistency in conceptualization.* After you have categorized the links, the next step is to facilitate a discussion about how individuals define themselves and others. Starting with "Concrete," proceed down the list of Hidalgo's categories, asking participants to raise their hands if they consider the items listed under that category to be the most important dimensions in how they define their own culture. Count the responses to each, and list them next to the category name on the board or paper. Using a graphing program

(or a protractor and ruler), have students create a pie chart that represents the responses for each of Hidalgo's three categories.

8. After sharing the pie charts, discuss the following with students:

- When you meet somebody, which of those items (under any of the categories) do you use to understand them culturally?
- Is your attempt to understand others culturally consistent with how you want to be viewed and understood?
- What forces in our society might contribute to our simplification of the culture of other's, even though we don't want to be defined simplistically ourselves?

9. *Wrapping up.* Divide the class into three groups and assign one of each of Hidalgo's three categories to each group. Have students design a piece of the pie chart by creating a visual representation of each of the categories. Students can cut out pictures from magazines, draw, or use any other medium they choose. Have each group present their piece of the pie to the class, with each "slice" being added until the pie is complete. Ask students from each group to comment about any difficulties they faced in representing each category in a visual way (a sample appears in Figure 1.3). (Note: The concrete piece will be easiest to do, simply by virtue of it consisting of visible elements; the behavioral and symbolic categories will be more challenging to properly represent visually. Discuss this fact with students in light of our tendency to make judgments about people based mainly on the concrete representations of culture that we see which, as highlighted by this activity, are not necessarily the deepest or truest revealers of culture/identity.)

Figure 1.3 Sample pie chart.

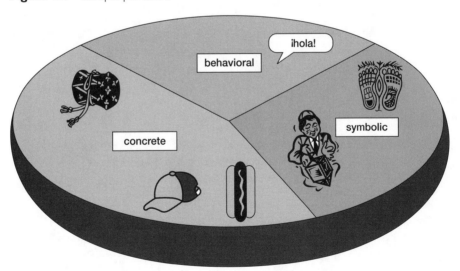

10. Have the class brainstorm an explanation of the activity in their own words. Display the explanation along with the pie chart in the classroom or hallway.

ACTION PROJECT

Conduct a survey of five friends, family members, teachers, or community members. Ask them to list as many of the dimensions of culture that they can think of. Keep a log of the responses and categorize the information using Hidalgo's levels of culture. Report your information and analysis back to the class. Create a class poster with the list of terms (both from your class activity and the survey) categorized into the three levels. Display your poster in the hallway or write a newspaper report about the project for your school newspaper.

REFLECTION

Which of Hildago's levels do you, as an educator, focus on when you are trying to teach multiculturally? How has education generally tried to be "multicultural"? What are the aspects or dimensions of culture that we focus on in our classrooms trying to be "multicultural"? Is this consistent with how we know people want to be defined?

Lesson 2 adapted from Paul C. Gorski's, *The Breadth and Depth of "Multicultural."* Used with permission.

LESSON 3

THE UNIVERSAL DECLARATION OF HUMAN RIGHTS

Go to the *Take Action!* DVD to view a video of this lesson, "The Universal Declaration of Human Rights," in action.

GRADE LEVELS

Grades 9–12

CONTENT AREAS ADDRESSED

History, Language Arts, Life Skills, Technology, World Language

TOPIC

The role of the United Nations (U.N.) in promoting human rights, diversity, international understanding, and humanitarian affairs through its U.N. convention. Discussion will focus on the Universal Declaration of Human Rights (UDHR) (see Lesson 3 Resource Page). Students will explore current violations of human rights in the form of lack of freedoms and economic and social inequalities.

RATIONALE FOR USING THIS LESSON

Students will be able to identify various obstacles and problems faced by different societies due to social, economical, and political crises. Students will gain knowledge of the Universal Declaration of Human Rights and its significance in establishing a culture of human rights and human security in society.

BACKGROUND INFORMATION: THE UNIVERSAL DECLARATION OF HUMAN RIGHTS

On December 10, 1948, the General Assembly of the United Nations adopted and proclaimed the Universal Declaration of Human Rights. Following this historic act, the Assembly called upon all member countries to publicize the text of the Declaration and "to cause it to be disseminated, displayed, read and expounded principally in schools and other educational institutions, without distinction based on the political status of countries or territories" (United Nations, 2007, n.p.). The preamble reads as follows:

> Whereas recognition of the inherent dignity and of the equal and inalienable rights of all members of the human family is the foundation of freedom, justice and peace in the world,
>
> Whereas disregard and contempt for human rights have resulted in barbarous acts which have outraged the conscience of mankind, and the advent of a world in which human beings shall enjoy freedom of speech and belief and freedom from fear and want has been proclaimed as the highest aspiration of the common people.

Whereas it is essential, if man is not to be compelled to have recourse, as a last resort, to rebellion against tyranny and oppression, that human rights should be protected by the rule of law,

Whereas it is essential to promote the development of friendly relations between nations,

Whereas the peoples of the United Nations have in the Charter reaffirmed their faith in fundamental human rights, in the dignity and worth of the human person and in the equal rights of men and women and have determined to promote social progress and better standards of life in larger freedom,

Whereas Member States have pledged themselves to achieve, in co-operation with the United Nations, the promotion of universal respect for and observance of human rights and fundamental freedoms,

Whereas a common understanding of these rights and freedoms is of the greatest importance for the full realization of this pledge,

Now, Therefore THE GENERAL ASSEMBLY proclaims THIS UNIVERSAL DECLARATION OF HUMAN RIGHTS as a common standard of achievement for all peoples and all nations, to the end that every individual and every organ of society, keeping this Declaration constantly in mind, shall strive by teaching and education to promote respect for these rights and freedoms and by progressive measures, national and international, to secure their universal and effective recognition and observance, both among the peoples of Member States themselves and among the peoples of territories under their jurisdiction.

The full text of the Universal Declaration of Human Rights appears on Lesson 3 Resource Page.

GOALS/AIMS

- Students will discuss and thus gain a deeper understanding of morals, ethics, human service, and equality.
- Students will gain an appreciation of and respect for diversity, and will gain a sense of community.
- Students will brainstorm, listen and share, reflect, order, compare/contrast, identify, and synthesize information.
- Students will participate in collaborative whole- and small-group discussion formats to share/discuss their ideas and understanding of the topic.
- Students will acknowledge, analyze, and appreciate each other's viewpoints.
- Students will create a class poster to present a summary of the key points regarding the group discussions.
- Students will participate in journal writing throughout the unit as a means of communicating their feelings, thoughts, and personal ideas that would otherwise go unnoticed (not shared) in an oral setting.

CONNECTIONS TO STANDARDS

- *Historical Understanding Standard 1:* Understands and knows how to analyze chronological relationships and patterns.
- *Historical Understanding Standard 2:* Understands the historical perspective. Analyzes the values held by specific people who influenced history and the role their values played in influencing history.
- *World History: Era 9—The 20th Century Since 1945:* Understands the search for community, stability, and peace in an interdependent world.

- *Language Arts Standard 7:* Uses reading skills and strategies to understand and interpret a variety of informational texts.
- *Life Skills—Working with others: Standard 1:* Contributes to the overall effort of a group.
- *Life Skills—Working with others: Standard 4:* Displays effective interpersonal communication skills.
- *Life Skills—Working with others: Standard 5:* Demonstrates leadership skills.
- *Technology Standard 1:* Knows the characteristics and uses of computer hardware and operating systems.
- *Technology Standard 2:* Knows the characteristics and uses of computer software programs.
- *World Language Standard 2:* Understands and interprets written and spoken language on diverse topics from diverse media.

(Copyright 2007. Reprinted with permission from *Content Knowledge: A Compendium of Standards and Benchmarks for K-12 Education,* 4th ed. http://www.mcrel.org/ standards-benchmarks/All rights reserved.)

MATERIALS

- Resource Page 3.1: The Universal Declaration of Human Rights
- Poster paper and markers
- Journals
- Case studies for in-class activity
- Internet access

ACTIVITY

1. *Brainstorm Session.* Ask students to brainstorm some of issues of diversity and/or social inequalities that our society faces. List all the responses on the board.
2. Have students review the brainstormed list. Ask them to talk about the ways in which the issues listed are harmful to our society. You might ask students to consider if the issues are ethical or detail how they might hurt our rights as U.S. citizens and/or as global citizens.
3. *The Universal Declaration of Human Rights.* Distribute a copy of the Universal Declaration of Human Rights to the students (Lesson 3 Resource Page). (Alternatively, provide students with the website for the UDHR (http://www.un.org/Overview/rights. html) and ask them to read it online. Encourage students who are studying a World Language to read a version of the UDHR in the language they are studying—there are over 300 different language versions available on the site.)
4. On the basis of the UDHR document, have students point out any human rights violations that they can link to some of the issues gleaned from the brainstorm. What rights are being violated?
5. *Research activity.* Have students work in pairs or small groups to research a particular violation—local or global—on the Internet. Have the student groups prepare a poster for the class that would include the topic (i.e., slavery), the setting (i.e., Mauritania), the specific UDHR right being violated (i.e., Article 4), and details/history about the issue. Encourage collaborative brainstorming with some member(s) of the group acting as a scribe(s) to synthesize information on the poster. Give students a time limit to discuss the issues and prepare posters. Presenters from each group will report the violations of the UDHR in their issues to the whole class via the use of their constructed poster.
6. *Journal writing.* Students will maintain a journal during the course of this lesson to reflect thoughts, feelings, and opinions about social inequality, violence, and so on.

CLOSE

Throughout this lesson, facilitate discussions, creating a safe, interactive dialogue between yourself and students as well as between students and students. Paraphrase student responses to highlight important concepts.

Teacher assessment includes the following:

- Student participation in the initial discussion of social inequality and violence
- Level of participation in the research activity
- Quality of journal entry writing
- Collaborative efforts in the poster-making activity
- Quality of presentation and level of knowledge and understanding of main themes

ACTION PROJECT

How can you get involved? Contact one of the agencies listed here and participate in a letter writing campaign, protest, or other activity. On each website, look for a link that reads "Take Action," or something of this nature.

- Amnesty International: http://www.amnesty.org/
- Human Rights Watch: http://www.hrw.org/
- One World: http://us.oneworld.net/
- Electronic Frontier Foundation: http://www.eff.org/
- International Action Center: http://www.iacenter.org/
- Anti-Slavery International: http://www.antislavery.org/

REFLECTION

How did students respond to the Universal Declaration of Human Rights? Were they surprised by any of the articles included in the document? If so, which ones? What kinds of issues did they document in their posters? Were most of the issues local or global? Why do you think this was the case?

Lesson 3 adapted from T. Nick IP's, *The Universal Declaration of Human Rights*. Used with permission.

LESSON 3 RESOURCE PAGE:
THE UNIVERSAL DECLARATION OF HUMAN RIGHTS

- *Article 1.* All human beings are born free and equal in dignity and rights. They are endowed with reason and conscience and should act towards one another in a spirit of brotherhood.

- *Article 2.* Everyone is entitled to all the rights and freedoms set forth in this Declaration, without distinction of any kind, such as race, colour, sex, language, religion, political or other opinion, national or social origin, property, birth or other status. Furthermore, no distinction shall be made on the basis of the political, jurisdictional or international status of the country or territory to which a person belongs, whether it be independent, trust, non-self-governing or under any other limitation of sovereignty.

- *Article 3.* Everyone has the right to life, liberty and security of person.

- *Article 4.* No one shall be held in slavery or servitude; slavery and the slave trade shall be prohibited in all their forms.

- *Article 5.* No one shall be subjected to torture or to cruel, inhuman or degrading treatment or punishment.

- *Article 6.* Everyone has the right to recognition everywhere as a person before the law.

- *Article 7.* All are equal before the law and are entitled without any discrimination to equal protection of the law. All are entitled to equal protection against any discrimination in violation of this Declaration and against any incitement to such discrimination.

- *Article 8.* Everyone has the right to an effective remedy by the competent national tribunals for acts violating the fundamental rights granted him by the constitution or by law.

- *Article 9.* No one shall be subjected to arbitrary arrest, detention or exile.

- *Article 10.* Everyone is entitled in full equality to a fair and public hearing by an independent and impartial tribunal, in the determination of his rights and obligations and of any criminal charge against him.

- *Article 11.* (1) Everyone charged with a penal offence has the right to be presumed innocent until proved guilty according to law in a public trial at which he has had all the guarantees necessary for his defense. (2) No one shall be held guilty of any penal offence on account of any act or omission which did not constitute a penal offence, under national or international law, at the time when it was committed. Nor shall a heavier penalty be imposed than the one that was applicable at the time the penal offence was committed.

- *Article 12.* No one shall be subjected to arbitrary interference with his privacy, family, home or correspondence, nor to attacks upon his honour and reputation. Everyone has the right to the protection of the law against such interference or attacks.

- *Article 13.* (1) Everyone has the right to freedom of movement and residence within the borders of each state. (2) Everyone has the right to leave any country, including his own, and to return to his country.

- *Article 14.* (1) Everyone has the right to seek and to enjoy in other countries asylum from persecution. (2) This right may not be invoked in the case of prosecutions genuinely arising from non-political crimes or from acts contrary to the purposes and principles of the United Nations.

- *Article 15.* (1) Everyone has the right to a nationality. (2) No one shall be arbitrarily deprived of his nationality nor denied the right to change his nationality.

- *Article 16.* (1) Men and women of full age, without any limitation due to race, nationality or religion, have the right to marry and to found a family. They are entitled to equal rights as to marriage, during marriage and at its dissolution. (2) Marriage shall be entered into only with the free and full consent of the intending spouses. (3) The family is the natural and fundamental group unit of society and is entitled to protection by society and the State.

- *Article 17.* (1) Everyone has the right to own property alone as well as in association with others. (2) No one shall be arbitrarily deprived of his property.

- *Article 18.* Everyone has the right to freedom of thought, conscience and religion; this right includes freedom to change his religion or belief, and freedom, either alone or in community with others and in public or private, to manifest his religion or belief in teaching, practice, worship and observance.

- *Article 19.* Everyone has the right to freedom of opinion and expression; this right includes freedom to hold opinions without interference and to seek, receive and impart information and ideas through any media and regardless of frontiers.

- *Article 20.* (1) Everyone has the right to freedom of peaceful assembly and association. (2) No one may be compelled to belong to an association.

- *Article 21.* (1) Everyone has the right to take part in the government of his country, directly or through freely chosen representatives. (2) Everyone has the right of equal access to public service in his country. (3) The will of the people shall be the basis of the authority of government; this will shall be expressed in periodic and genuine elections which shall be by universal and equal suffrage and shall be held by secret vote or by equivalent free voting procedures.

- *Article 22.* Everyone, as a member of society, has the right to social security and is entitled to realization, through national effort and international co-operation and in accordance with the organization and resources of each State, of the economic, social and cultural rights indispensable for his dignity and the free development of his personality.

- *Article 23.* (1) Everyone has the right to work, to free choice of employment, to just and favourable conditions of work and to protection against unemployment. (2) Everyone, without any discrimination, has the right to equal pay for equal work. (3) Everyone who works has the right to just and favourable remuneration ensuring for himself and his family an existence worthy of human dignity, and supplemented, if necessary, by other means of social protection. (4) Everyone has the right to form and to join trade unions for the protection of his interests.

- *Article 24.* Everyone has the right to rest and leisure, including reasonable limitation of working hours and periodic holidays with pay.

- *Article 25.* (1) Everyone has the right to a standard of living adequate for the health and well-being of himself and of his family, including food, clothing, housing and medical care and necessary social services, and the right to security in the event of unemployment, sickness, disability, widowhood, old age or other lack of livelihood in circumstances beyond his control. (2) Motherhood and childhood are entitled to special care and assistance. All children, whether born in or out of wedlock, shall enjoy the same social protection.

- *Article 26.* (1) Everyone has the right to education. Education shall be free, at least in the elementary and fundamental stages. Elementary education shall be compulsory. Technical and professional education shall be made generally available and higher education shall be equally accessible to all on the basis of merit. (2) Education shall be directed to the full development of the human personality and to the strengthening of respect for human rights and fundamental freedoms. It shall promote understanding, tolerance and friendship among all nations, racial or religious groups, and shall further the activities of the United Nations for the maintenance of peace. (3) Parents have a prior right to choose the kind of education that shall be given to their children.

- *Article 27.* (1) Everyone has the right freely to participate in the cultural life of the community, to enjoy the arts and to share in scientific advancement and its benefits. (2) Everyone has the right to the protection of the moral and material interests resulting from any scientific, literary or artistic production of which he is the author.

- ***Article 28.*** Everyone is entitled to a social and international order in which the rights and freedoms set forth in this Declaration can be fully realized.
- ***Article 29.*** (1) Everyone has duties to the community in which alone the free and full development of his personality is possible. (2) In the exercise of his rights and freedoms, everyone shall be subject only to such limitations as are determined by law solely for the purpose of securing due recognition and respect for the rights and freedoms of others and of meeting the just requirements of morality, public order and the general welfare in a democratic society. (3) These rights and freedoms may in no case be exercised contrary to the purposes and principles of the United Nations.
- ***Article 30.*** Nothing in this Declaration may be interpreted as implying for any State, group or person any right to engage in any activity or to perform any act aimed at the destruction of any of the rights and freedoms set forth herein.

United Nations. (2007). The Universal Declaration of Human Rights. Retrieved June 11, 2007 from http://www.un.org/Overview/rights.html

CHAPTER 2

CULTURE AND IDENTITY

Culture is an elusive construct that shifts constantly over time and according to who is perceiving and interpreting it.

L. HARKLAU, Representing culture in the ESL writing classroom. In E. Hinkel (Ed.),
Culture in second language teaching and learning (pp. 109–130). New York:
Cambridge University Press, 1999.

Some Background

So much of our daily lives—our attitudes towards work and play, the relationships we have, our perspectives regarding what is good and bad—is tied to our identity. We tend to build an image of ourselves and this image forms a lens through which we see the world around us. Often, we view identity as a static entity. We are prone to describing ourselves in terms that are monolithic and stable. Yet identity is actually a fluid, ever-changing thing. It shifts over time. Just think of the changes you have experienced from childhood to adulthood. Identity changes depending on our environment. For example, think about how differently you feel and behave when at home and when you are far away from its comforts. Identity also changes depending on who we interact with. Consider how differently you communicate with your boss versus with your best friend.

Culture is similarly fluid in nature. How do most people define culture? It can be linked to one's ethnic background or race. It might have to do with religion, or with sexual orientation. It might be closely linked to your social group, the music you listen to, or your profession. Like identity, one's culture can change with the time, place, or company we keep. It is ever evolving and developing.

Despite being difficult to define in definite terms, the cultures and identities of both students and teachers greatly affect the classroom environment. For this reason, it is important to "take the temperature" of students at the start of the school year to get a feel for how they self-identify and what elements of culture are important to them. This is important for several reasons. First of all, this type of activity can set a tone of openness and respect in your classroom right from the very start. Also, by doing this as soon as the year begins, you can avoid the very natural categorization that teachers engage in as a means of making sense of the diverse student body. We all want to understand our students and get to know them as individuals. If students are not forthcoming and do not share "who they are," we tend to make our own decisions about them. By allowing students to talk about themselves—and by engaging in that dialogue yourself as the teacher—you validate each individual's right to self-identify and to lay claim to their own definitions. This type of sharing can be very powerful in establishing a multicultural classroom.

Lesson Preparation for the Teacher

ONE TEACHER'S REFLECTION—WHO AM I?

At the age of 17, my mother was forced to divulge a secret that she had hoped never to reveal. My sister had been out with a neighbor from down the block, who was fairly mean spirited and enjoyed teasing us. She had always said that we were adopted, but since this was a common put-down among children, we took it more as a derogatory statement than a revelation. Jill came in to the house to get a drink and casually asked Mom if we were adopted. I'll never forget the look on my mother's face as 17 years of lies suddenly crumbled and she started to cry. She took us to my sister's room, sat us down on her pale yellow and green-striped bedspread and said, "It's true. You are both adopted."

Jill thought for a moment and went back outside to play. She had inherited my father's characteristic lack of emotion. I, on the other hand, broke down in tears, though I didn't know why at the time. I was most confused that it didn't hurt me to hear that the woman sitting in tears next to me was not my biological mother. I had already spent 17 years convinced that she was my birth mother and I felt that it was too late for me to think otherwise.

Later, after I had time to think, I began to ask the obvious questions: Am I Jewish? Am I Russian like my Grandma? Is my real name Joy? Where do I come from? Mom was in no shape to answer me and I decided not to push, but Jill would sneak into Mom's drawers when she was out, looking for adoption papers and information about her own identity.

Jill found her adoption papers and soon discovered that she was Irish, French, and Swedish. Ever since this discovery, I send Jill a Saint Patrick's Day card, as a little nod to her "new" ethnic identity. It was much later that I found a small clipping from my own papers. I found my birth mother's name and some information about her and my birth father. My father was of Italian descent and my mother of Irish and German heritage. My father was a photographer and I get my asthma from him. My mother played the guitar and made her living as a teacher! This is amazing to me, even as I sit and think about it today. It's incredible how linked the profession of teaching is to my life.

I decided not to look for my parents, as many adopted children choose to do. At first this was a decision made mainly with my mother in mind. Mom was terrified that she would lose my sister and me and for that reason chose not to tell us that we were adopted. It was only after she felt that she had no choice that she revealed this truth to us and I felt that I would hurt her and I'd prove disloyal by searching for someone who was, in all reality, a stranger. I may search some time in the future for this person who gave birth to me. I would like to see what she looks like and learn about our medical history.

Growing up, I didn't really feel Jewish or Russian. As a young adult about to start college, I couldn't very well learn to be German-Irish or Italian. Is ethnic identity linked to biology or environment? Do I have a right to choose one of those identities, or am I some combination of all of them?

TEACHER ACTION PROJECT: DISSECTING DEFINITIONS

We have all heard the talk in the teacher's lounge at the start of the school year: "Oh! You have Tim H. in your class this year? Watch out! He's a handful. He's got ants in his pants in the classroom, but is super-lazy at home. Smart boy, but an underachiever. I wish you luck with that one." How much does that short interaction with a colleague color your subsequent relationship with Tim H.? It is always fascinating to learn about a student's identity through the eyes of others. It is even more eye-opening to explore a student's identity through his own eyes.

Choose one student that you don't already know much about. Perhaps you noticed the student in the hallways for whatever reason: exotic dress, a Mohawk hairstyle, she's particularly shy and sad looking, or very pretty and popular. Ask the student if it would be all right to interview her about her identity. Possible questions include the following:

- How would you define your identity?
- How would you define your culture?
- What things are most important to you?
- What do you want your teachers to think about when they hear your name?
- What do you want your friends to think about when they hear your name?

Ask the student if she wouldn't mind you talking to her former teachers. Assure her that this activity is just for your own information, and that no report or other data will be revealed to parents, teachers, or other students. If she agrees, interview three former (or current) teachers about the student. Possible questions include:

- How would you define the student's identity?
- How would you define the student's culture?
- What things are most important to the student?
- What do you think of when you hear the student's name?

Review the responses to your questions from the different sources. Do the teachers' responses match the student's? In what ways do the student's identities mesh with what the teachers revealed? In what ways are they different? How might have the teachers' impressions of the student's identity affected her relationship with them? How might they have affected her performance in class?

If you feel comfortable, share your results with the student and/or the teachers.

References and Suggested Readings

Bayart, J-F. (2005). *The illusion of cultural identity.* Chicago: University of Chicago Press.

Berry, J. W. (Ed.). (2006). *Immigrant youth in cultural transition: Acculturation, identity, and adaptation across national contexts.* Mahwah, NJ: Lawrence Erlbaum Associates.

Boyd, D. (2006). Identity production in a networked culture: Why youth heart MySpace. American Association for the Advancement of Science. Talk given February 19, 2006. Retrieved July 10, 2006 from http://www.danah.org/papers/AAAS2006.html

Chickering, A. W., & Reisser, L. (1993). *Education and identity.* San Francisco: Jossey-Bass.

Eckert, P. (1989). *Jocks and burnouts: Social categories and identity in the high school.* New York: Teachers College Press.

Edgerton, S. H. (1996). *Translating the curriculum: Multiculturalism into cultural studies.* New York: Routledge.

Freire, P. (2006). *Teachers as cultural workers: Letters to those who dare teach.* Boulder, CO: Westview.

Hall, S. (Ed.). (1996). *Questions of cultural identity.* Thousand Oaks, CA: Sage.

Hollins, E. (1996). *Culture in school learning: Revealing the deep meaning.* Mahwah, NJ: Lawrence Erlbaum Associates.

Lindsey, R. B., Roberts, L. M., & Campbell-Jones, F. (2004). *The culturally proficient school: An implementation guide for school leaders.* Thousand Oaks, CA: Corwin.

Mody, S. L. (2005). *Cultural identity in kindergarten: A study of Asian Indian children in New Jersey.* New York: Routledge, Taylor & Francis.

Sadowski, M. (Ed.). (2003). *Adolescents at school: Perspectives on youth, identity, and education.* Cambridge, MA: Harvard Education.

Seelye, H. N., & Wasilewski, J. H. (1996). *Between cultures: Developing self-identity in a world of diversity.* New York: McGraw-Hill.

Sleeter, C. (2005). *Culture, difference, and power.* New York: Teachers College Press.

Woodward, K. (Ed.). (1997). *Identity and difference (Culture, media and identities series).* Thousand Oaks, CA: Sage.

LESSON 4

NAME STORIES

Grades K–5

CONTENT AREAS ADDRESSED

Language Arts, Life Skills, Visual Arts

TOPIC

Sharing the source of one's names. This activity works toward bringing the stories of individuals to the fore in the multicultural experience.

RATIONALE FOR USING THIS LESSON

Names—given names and family names—often reveal a great deal about a person's cultural background or identity. By encouraging students to share their names with the class, you can begin to establish an open and accepting classroom environment while validating the individual identities and cultures of each student.

BACKGROUND INFORMATION: NAMES AND PERSONAL IDENTITY

Names are a part of every culture and they are of enormous importance both to the people who receive names and to the societies that give them.

Despite their universality, there is a great deal of difference from one culture to another in how names are given. Among most preliterate peoples, names are determined according to very definite and specific rules. Generally, in cultures with a keen sense of ancestry, children get their names from the totems and family trees of their parents. In some cultures, names are taken from events that happen during the pregnancy of the mother or shortly after the birth of the child. In others, names are divined through magic and incantation. In some cases, the name given at birth is only the first of several names a person will bear throughout life. When this happens, the new names are given either to mark important milestones in life or to ward off evil spirits by tricking them into thinking that the person with the old name has disappeared.

Regardless of when, why, or how often it happens, though, the giving and receiving of a name is an event of major importance. Quite frequently the significance of names is emphasized by elaborate rituals that almost always have deep religious meaning. One rather dramatic example of this is the naming ceremony of the Khasi people in Africa. Among these people, children are named within a day of their births. The ceremony begins when a relative of the child prepares a sacrifice by pouring rice meal into small dishes and filling a gourd with rice liquor. After an invocation, the relative pours the liquor into the rice meal while reciting a list of names. The name the child will have is the one the relative recites during the pouring of the drop of liquor that takes the longest to leave the bottle. Once the name is "discovered" in this way, they anoint the baby's feet with the meal-and-liquor paste, and the parents and relatives eat the paste. Then, after swinging it over the baby three times, the father leaves the group to bury the placenta (Charles, 1951).

In the Catholic baptismal ceremony, the priest meets the parents, godparents, and baby at the door of the church building, and the first thing he says is, "What name do you give your child?" After the parents answer this and other questions, the priest invites the parents and godparents to trace the sign of the cross on the child's forehead, and then they move into the main body of the building for the rest of the christening.

In industrialized countries, parents must register a child's birth and record the child's name. In this way, the child's name becomes part of the public record of the society. The birth certificate the parents receive when they register the child's birth becomes a kind of ticket or passport to some of the essential services the society offers its members. For example, public schools in the United States require that prospective students present birth certificates when they register for classes. If a child doesn't have a birth certificate for some reason, the school system feels no obligation toward the child until the parents produce a birth certificate or provide some other type of verification of the child's legal name and date of birth.

The names parents choose for their children also reflect the relationship between name and identity that the symbolic contract seals. This is particularly true of the names of twins, for whom the establishment of a unique identity is often difficult. Parents tend to think of twins as a single person who happens to have two bodies, and they often choose names for them that reinforce the idea that the twins have a single, shared identity.

We find an awareness of the link between name and identity in everyday speech, particularly in the words we use in making introductions and in identifying ourselves when we answer the telephone. When we introduce ourselves, we usually say something like, "Hi. I'm John Mendoza," and when we answer the phone we probably say something like, "Hello. This is Swati Patel speaking." Occasionally, before a group of strangers, we might use a more distant form and say, "My name is Omar Lateef, and I work . . .," but we almost always reserve this style for situations where our function or job is more important than who we really *are*. On the other hand, we would probably never answer the phone by saying, "Hello. My name is Susan Jones," nor would we introduce someone else with an expression like, "Mother, this person's name is Beth." The reason we instinctively choose "I am . . ." or "This is . . ." is that we intuitively associate our identity and the identity of the person we are introducing with a name.

The same idea applies when our name is mispronounced. Most people take great care to make sure they pronounce another person's name correctly, especially in introductions. The reason for this concern is that people generally resent the mispronunciation of their name because mispronunciation amounts to a distortion of their identity. Accidental distortions are annoying, but mispronunciations and distortions of a name on purpose are sizable insults, especially if they result in unflattering puns. Martin Luther used this tactic to belittle one of his enemies, Dr. Eck, by purposely writing his name as Dreck, which means filth.

The sense of personal identity and uniqueness that a name gives us is at the heart of why names interest us and why they are important to us as individuals and to our society as a whole. In spite of their importance, though, most people know very little about names and about the effects they have on us and on our children in everyday life. In a very real sense, we are consumers of names, and we have a need and right to know about the psychological, magical, legal, religious, and ethnic aspects of our names.

(Copyright © 1996 by H. Edward Deluzain. Reprinted by permission.)

References

Charles, L. H. (1951). Drama in first-naming ceremonies. *Journal of American Folklore, 64,* 11–35.

GOALS/AIMS

- Students will be able to appreciate cultures different than their own.
- Students will understand that names have many meanings and sources.

CONNECTIONS TO STANDARDS

- *Language Arts Writing Standard 1:* Uses general skills and strategies of the writing process.
- *Language Arts Listening and Speaking Standard 8:* Uses listening and speaking strategies for different purposes.
- *Life Skills—Working with others: Standard 4:* Displays effective interpersonal communication skills.
- *Visual Arts Standard 1:* Understands and applies media, techniques, and processes related to the visual arts.
- *Visual Arts Standard 4:* Understands the visual arts in relation to history and cultures.

(Copyright 2007. Reprinted with permission from Content Knowledge: A Compendium of Standards
and Benchmarks for K-12 Education, 4th ed. http://www.mcrel.org/standards-benchmarks/
All rights reserved.)

MATERIALS

- Large index cards (5" × 8" size works best), enough for every student
- Markers or crayons

ACTIVITY

1. Ask participants to write short (1–2 page) stories about their names (you may have to assign this prior to the class). Leave the assignment open to individual interpretation as much as possible, but if asked for more specific instructions, suggest some or all of the following possibilities:

   - Who gave you your name? Why?
   - What is the ethnic origin of your name?
   - Does your name mean something in a language other than English?
   - What are your nicknames, if any?
   - What do you prefer to be called?

   Encourage students to be creative. They might write poetry, include humor, list adjectives that describe themselves, and so on. Also, be sure to let them know that they will be sharing their stories with the rest of the class. (Note: For younger/preliterate students, have them think about and tell their stories orally, rather than in writing.)

Read this sample story to students (or use one about your own name):

According to my mother, "Paul" means "small." My parents wanted to name me "Cameron." "Paul" goes back three or four generations. My father and his father and his father are all named "Paul." But my mother liked "Cameron," so "Cameron" it was. But then I was born . . . five weeks prematurely. I was a tiny baby. I was the itsy-bitsiest baby in the new baby room at the hospital. According to my mother, that was a sign. Remember, "Paul" means "small."

So I am Paul Cameron Gorski. My father is Paul Peter Gorski. The problem is when someone calls my parents' home for one of us. At that point we become Big Paul and Little Paul, the father Paul and the son Paul. Sometimes people call and I'm too tired to explain to them the whole idea that there are two Pauls living in one house, so I just pretend to be Paul Peter, and give my Dad the message later. He doesn't seem to mind that, especially when the caller is trying to sell us something. Still, I hope he doesn't do the same thing.

Paul lends itself well to rhyming nicknames. Bill, a good friend of mine, calls me "Tall Paul." He's being silly, of course, because I am really short. The truth of the matter is that I really don't know whether or not "Paul" means "small." Perhaps it means "Jedi warrior" or "sunflower" or "straight A student." No matter. I've never looked it up, and never will. According to my Mom, "Paul" means "small." That sounds good to me.

2. To ensure that everybody has an opportunity to share their story, break into diverse small groups of three to four students. Give participants the option to either read their stories or to share their stories from memory. Ask for volunteers to share their stories. Points to remember:

   • Because some individuals will include very personal information, some may be hesitant to read them, even in small groups. It is sometimes effective in such situations for facilitators to share their stories first. If you make yourself vulnerable, others will be more comfortable doing the same.

   • Be sure to allow time for everyone to be able to speak, whether reading their stories or sharing them from memory.

   • When everyone has shared, ask participants how it felt to share their stories. Why is this activity important? What did you learn?

3. Give each student an index card. Have them fold it lengthwise with the lined side on the inside. Ask them to write/draw their given first name on one side (i.e., the name that is on file with the school as their "official" first name). On the other side, ask students to write/draw the name that they would like to be called in class. (Note: you may have to help younger/preliterate students write their names; also, you may have to lay some ground rules for this part as to what names/words are acceptable in the classroom.)

4. Ask students to decorate their cards (both sides) with some form of decoration that reveals their likes or personalities. Have students keep their name cards on their desks.

ACTION PROJECT

Have students interview adults about their names. Students should choose one family member, one teacher, and one community member to tell them the story of their names. After collecting information about three adults, have students create a name card for one adult, using information from the name story to decorate the card. Encourage the students to give the card to the person as a gift and a "thank you" for sharing their story. As a class, create a "Book of Names" with a page for each of the stories that students wrote and collected.

REFLECTION

Prior to the start of the school year, when you look at your class list for the first time, what assumptions do you make about your students based on their names? Are their certain names that automatically make you feel angry? Happy? Confident? Fearful? How do your reactions to students' names affect your interactions with them in the classroom?

Lesson 4 adapted from Paul C. Gorski's, *Name Stories*. Used with permission.

LESSON 5

DEFINING CULTURE

GRADE LEVELS

Grades 6–8

CONTENT AREAS ADDRESSED

Language Arts, Life Skills, World Languages, Visual Arts

TOPIC

Students will define the word *culture* by looking through different lenses at the meaning of the word on a personal level.

RATIONALE FOR USING THIS LESSON

Through defining "culture" for themselves, students will develop an understanding of the elements that make up culture and an appreciation for the different cultures that exist in society.

BACKGROUND INFORMATION: "BIG C" AND "LITTLE c" CULTURE

What is culture? Culture is a complex of myriad human designs for existence. Definitions and perceptions abound about this word that describes behaviors, mores, traditions, and customs that everyone is likely to understand without definition. The Latin origin of the word is *colore*, which means to cultivate, to honor or to inhabit. One definition by McCarthy (1994) explains that "culture can be generally defined as the set of values and beliefs that are prevalent within a given society or section of a society" (pg. 150). This definition takes on features similar to those mentioned above. McCarthy refers as well to two perspectives about culture: "Big C" and "Small c" culture, and goes on to include "culture as social discourse" (pg. 151). The first of these cultural perspectives ("Big C") typically refers to the great achievements and events of the society, as well as its geographical characteristics, historical events, leaders, major cities, products, artistic achievements, religions and ceremonies, among other features. "Small c" culture covers just about everything else, particularly characteristics and activities of the people who make up the culture. The two characterizations of culture are bridged by the third, "social discourse," since one could hardly engage in natural human discourse within a society without dealing with matters which are part of the cultural life.

In defining a "social community," Kramsch (1995) indicates that the humanities tend to concentrate on material productions of the community: the arts, literature, institutions, grand achievements, etc. (These fall under the "Big C" categorization of culture mentioned previously.) Reflected in such a broad perspective of culture are the attitudes and beliefs, ways of thinking and general and common behaviors of the individuals who make up the culture.

(From Gurney, D. W. (2005). Culture, Language and the Brain. Retrieved June 12, 2007 from http://pegasus.cc.ucf.edu/~gurney/CultXcpts.doc)

References

Kramsch, C. (1995). Rhetorical models of understanding. In T. Miller (ed.) *Functional Approaches to Written Texts: Classroom Applications*. Paris: TESOL-France.

McCarthy, C. (1994). Multicultural discourses and curriculum reform: A critical perspective. *Educational Theory, 44*(1), 150–151.

GOALS/AIMS

- Students will be able to define the term *culture*.
- Students will be able to recognize different characteristics that make up a culture.
- Students will be able to make connections between the term *culture* and their own lives.
- Students will develop an appreciation for diversity and multiculturalism.
- Students will be able to present a report to the class.
- Students will be able to work in small groups.

CONNECTIONS TO STANDARDS

- *Language Arts Writing Standard 1:* Uses general skills and strategies of the writing process.
- *Language Arts Reading Standard 7:* Uses reading skills and strategies to understand and interpret a variety of informational texts.
- *Language Arts Listening and Speaking Standard 8:* Uses listening and speaking strategies for different purposes.
- *Life Skills—Working with others: Standard 1:* Contributes to the overall effort of a group.
- *Life Skills—Working with others: Standard 4:* Displays effective interpersonal communication skills.
- *Life Skills—Working with others: Standard 5:* Demonstrates leadership skills.
- *Visual Arts Standard 1:* Understands and applies media, techniques, and processes related to the visual arts.
- *World Language Standard 5:* Understands that different languages use different patterns to communicate and applies this knowledge to the target and native languages.

(Copyright 2007. Reprinted with permission from *Content Knowledge: A Compendium of Standards and Benchmarks for K-12 Education,* 4th ed. http://www.mcrel.org/standards-benchmarks/ All rights reserved.)

MATERIALS

- Lesson 5 Resource Page 1: *Colore* Brainstorming Chart
- Lesson 5 Resource Page 2: Culture Cube Template
- Art supplies: markers, paints, magazines, scissors, glue
- Access to a computer with the Internet (optional—for clip art resources, if necessary)

1. *Motivation:* Begin class by asking students to define the word *culture.* Write students' responses on the board.

2. After the class is satisfied with their answers, explain to students that the Latin root of *culture* is *colere,* which means three things:
   a. To honor
   b. To inhabit
   c. To cultivate

   As a class, lead a discussion in which students offer explanations and examples for these three meanings. For example:
   a. To honor: a person shows respect to someone or something from the past
   b. To inhabit: to live somewhere
   c. To cultivate: when someone cultivates a plant, they care for it, grow it, harvest it

   List synonyms and phrases on the board next to each term as students come up with explanations and ideas.

3. In small groups, have students brainstorm how their first definitions of *culture* might connect to the Latin root for the word. For example, part of a student's culture might involve *honoring* her ancestors. After students have time to record their thoughts, share them with the class.

4. You might need to help students to make connections among the definitions and different aspects of culture and personal idenity. Examples of how to explain these connections to your students:
   a. To honor: Cultures often involve respect for historical events, ancestors, and traditions. A large part of one's cultural identity involves honoring the past or history of one's family, home, language, religion, and so on. Honoring also deals with values. What a person values in life is part of one's cultural identity.
   b. To inhabit: Culture sometimes has to do with geography. For example, your family may come from South America, but you live in the United States. Both South America (your family's original home) and your current home (the United States) affect your cultural identity. Geography can also be as local as neighborhood or region.
   c. To cultivate: Sometimes we create our own culture. For example, a student may come from a home in which parents listen to classical music, but the student has developed a love for jazz. This is a cultivated aspect of the student's cultural identity. In a sense, we all cultivate some parts of our cultural identity when our tastes or interests become important. Some people's love for dogs is so strong that they call themselves "dog people" (versus "cat people" for example)—this is very much a part of that person's identity.

5. Give students a copy of Lesson 5 Resource Page 1. Ask students to think about their own culture and how the three meanings of the Latin root word might relate to their own lives. Have them list words that describe their own cultural identity for each of the three terms.

6. Using the information from their brainstorm sheet, have students design their own "culture cube" by filling in each of the three spaces with images that reflect their cultural identity. (Lesson 5 Resource Page 2 provides a template.) They might draw these images, use clip art from the computer, or cut pictures out of magazines. Encourage students to also include photos and/or artifacts (i.e., ticket stubs, playbills, etc.) from their own lives.

7. Have students present their cubes orally to the class. They should explain each division of their cube and tell about the images they chose to represent each aspect of culture.

ACTION PROJECT

In a large group, create one large "culture cube" for the class. Students might be divided into three groups with each group taking one element to develop. The cube should demonstrate what the class honors (i.e., hard work, honesty, etc.), where the school "lives" (i.e., the neighborhood, region, etc.), and what the class cultivates (i.e., independent reading, critical thinking skills, etc.). Piece the three elements together and display the cube in the room. Another cube could be created for the school as a whole, or the district.

REFLECTION

Were students able to articulate their own cultural identity in writing? Was is any easier for them to do so visually? What (if anything) did you learn about your students from this activity that you didn't know before doing the lesson? Did the definitions of *culture* change your own thinking about the term?

Lesson 5 adapted from Yelena Patish's, *Creating Culture*. Used with permission.

LESSON 5 RESOURCE PAGE 1: COLORE BRAINSTORMING CHART

CULTURE

Latin root: *Colore*

To Inhabit	To Cultivate	To Honor

LESSON 5 RESOURCE PAGE 2:
CULTURE CUBE TEMPLATE

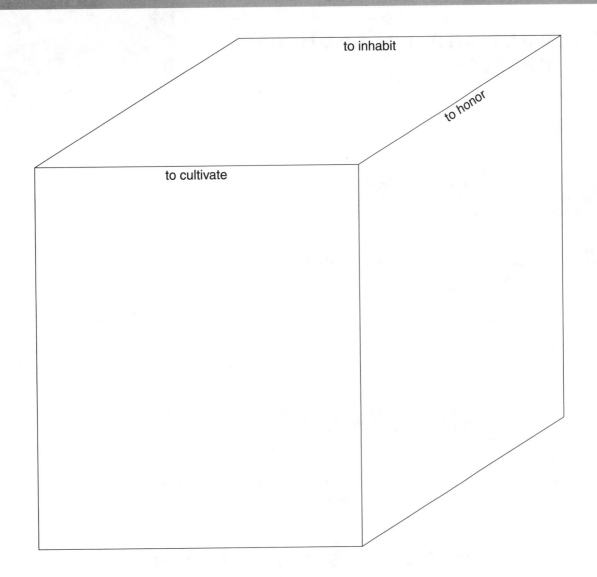

to inhabit

to honor

to cultivate

LESSON 6

SCHOOLS AND FREEDOM OF EXPRESSION

Go to the Take Action! DVD to view a video of this lesson, "Schools and Freedom of Expression," in action.

GRADE LEVELS

Grades 9–12

CONTENT AREAS ADDRESSED

Civics, Language Arts, Life Skills, Technology, Visual Arts

TOPIC

Students will discuss the ways in which clothing reveals a person's culture and identity as part of a debate on the issues surrounding school uniforms.

RATIONALE FOR USING THIS LESSON

Clothing is an important part of the self-expression of almost every teenager. It is used to reveal personal identity and expression of everything from tastes in music to religious beliefs. By allowing students to debate the issue of mandatory school uniforms, you can also open up a valuable discussion about individualism, identity, and culture as it is revealed through clothing choice.

BACKGROUND INFORMATION: SCHOOL UNIFORMS

A policy recently rising in popularity is school uniforms. A recent study by the U.S. Department of Education suggests that school uniforms can help reduce theft, violence, and the negative effects of peer pressure caused when some students come to school wearing designer clothing and expensive sneakers. A uniform code also prevents gang members from wearing colors and insignia that could cause trouble and helps school officials recognize intruders who do not belong on campus.

In Long Beach, California, students, teachers, parents, and school officials worked together to establish a uniform code for all elementary and middle schools. Each school chooses what its uniform will look like. In addition, students can "opt out" of wearing a uniform if they have their parents' approval. The Long Beach program involves 58,000 students and includes assistance for families that cannot afford to buy uniforms. In many Long Beach schools, graduating students donate or sell their used uniforms to needy families.

In the year following the establishment of the uniform policy, Long Beach school officials found that overall school crime decreased 36 percent. Fights decreased 51 percent, sex offenses decreased 74 percent, weapons offenses decreased 50 percent, assault and battery offenses decreased 34 percent, and vandalism decreased 18 percent. Less than 1 percent of the students chose not to wear uniforms.

Across the country, the adoption of school uniforms is so new that it's impossible to tell whether it will have a long-term impact on school violence. Critics have doubts. And some parents, students, and educators find uniforms coercive and demeaning. Some students complain that uniforms turn schools into prisons.

(From Constitutional Rights Foundation. (2007). School uniforms—The challenge of school violence. Retrieved June 12, 2007 from http://www.crf-usa.org/violence/school.html)

GOALS/AIMS

- Students will be able to analyze elements of expression that reveal cultural identity.
- Students will debate recent court cases in which clothing and identity intersect in problematic ways.
- Students will apply understanding of constitutional law to current court cases.
- Students will debate the validity of a dress code for their own school.
- Students will design their own class dress code in small groups.

CONNECTIONS TO STANDARDS

- *Civics Standard 9: What Are the Basic Values and Principals of American Democracy:* Understands the role of diversity in American life and the importance of shared values, political beliefs, and civic beliefs in an increasingly diverse American society.
- *Language Arts Writing Standard 1:* Uses general skills and strategies of the writing process.
- *Language Arts Reading Standard 7:* Uses reading skills and strategies to understand and interpret a variety of informational texts.
- *Language Arts Listening and Speaking Standard 8:* Uses listening and speaking strategies for different purposes.
- *Life Skills Standards—Working with others: Standard 1:* Contributes to the overall effort of a group.
- *Life Skills Standards—Working with others: Standard 4:* Displays effective interpersonal communication skills.
- *Life Skills Standards—Working with others: Standard 5:* Demonstrates leadership skills.
- *Technology Standard 1:* Knows the characteristics and uses of computer hardware and operating systems.
- *Technology Standard 2:* Knows the characteristics and uses of computer software programs.
- *Visual Arts Standard 1:* Understands and applies media, techniques, and processes related to the visual arts.
- *Visual Arts Standard 4:* Understands the visual arts in relation to history and cultures.

(Copyright 2007. Reprinted with permission from *Content Knowledge: A Compendium of Standards and Benchmarks for K-12 Education,* 4th ed. http://www.mcrel.org/standards-benchmarks/ All rights reserved.)

MATERIALS

- Art materials:
  - Large, white, unlined paper
  - Crayons, markers, or paints
  - Fabric swatches
  - Magazines for cutting out pictures
  - Glue
  - Scissors

ACTIVITY

1. Have the class brainstorm the word *identity*. Ask them to think about all the ways in which we express our identity in public. One of the visual elements of identity is dress, or clothing. This term will most likely come out of the brainstorm. If it doesn't, help students to think about this expression of identity. Write student responses on the board.

2. Focus students in on the element of dress and ask them to brainstorm in small groups all the ways in which dress can reveal one's identity or culture. Have each group share their ideas with the class.

3. In small groups, have students read several dress code court cases in which students were censored or banned for wearing certain types of clothing to school. Here are four possible cases (more can be found on the American Civil Liberties website: http://www.aclu.org/studentsrights/dresscodes/index.html):

   CASE 1: Male high school student wore a tee shirt to school with an anarchy symbol. He was suspended for 5 days. He had already been given detention three times for wearing peace symbols, upside-down American Flags, and antiwar slogans. On all three prior occasions, he refused to change. He was warned the last time that the next time he wore something "inappropriate" the school would suspend him.

   CASE 2: Student wore a tee shirt with a picture of President Bush and the words "International Terrorist." He was asked by the principal to remove the shirt, turn it inside out, or go home. He refused all options and was suspended.

   CASE 3: Just after 9/11 an American Muslim female student in high school was asked to stop wearing her hijab to school for her own safety. She refused to take it off and was sent home.

   CASE 4: In Utah, a high school Gay–Straight Alliance designed a tee shirt for Kick Butts Day that said "Queers Kick Ash." They were told if they wore the shirts, the school would cancel their club for the rest of the year. They wore the shirts anyway. Three homosexual boys were immediately suspended and had it marked on their records. One heterosexual girl was sent home without suspension being placed on her record.

4. For each case, have students report the following information to the rest of the class:

   - Constitutional issue(s), citing specific amendment(s) from the Bill of Rights or articles of the Constitution.
   - Give both sides/perspectives of the issue.
   - How would you decide if you were the judge in the case?
   - How does the situation affect the "identity" of the students involved?

FOLLOW-UP ACTIVITY

Set up a debate in which one group is in favor of a dress code or uniforms for your school and one group is opposed. Give students time to research information online or in the library to support their side of the argument.

No matter what side wins the debate, continue the discussion by having each side create a design to support their ideas:

1. The pro–dress code side should design a uniform for the school. They can use markers, paints, magazine cutouts, or even swatches of fabric. Their design for a school uniform should include elements that reflect the culture of students in the school.

2. Have the opposing side design a dress code by creating a list of appropriate clothing and inappropriate or unacceptable clothing for the school. Again, this "code" should be inclusive of all the different cultures that are represented in the school.

    Have each side present their designs/list to the class.

ACTION PROJECT

Have students research other schools online that have a dress code or use school uniforms. Ask them to contact and interview, via email, a school official regarding the policy, students' reactions, and parents' feelings. Using information gleaned from the interviews, the debate, and the online cases, have students create a class position paper for your own school principal or policy committee regarding the issue of dress code/school uniforms. Present the report at a student council or student government meeting.

REFLECTION

How do you feel about a dress code or school uniforms for students? What elements of your own identity and/or culture do you express through your dress? Should teachers have a dress code? If so, what might it look like? Have you ever felt that one of your students was ever inappropriately dressed in school? What about one of your colleagues?

Lesson 6 adapted from Jodi Thompson's, *"Schools and Freedom of Expression."* Used with permission.

CHAPTER 3

RACE AND ETHNICITY

*We've got Chinese, white, black and mixed; but remember that our colors
are cheap, for after many years of contracts and tricks nobody's purity
runs very deep.*

NICOLÁS GUILLÉN (Cuban poet, 1902–1989)

Some Background

When one thinks about multicultural education and diversity in schools, race and ethnicity are two concepts that often spring to mind. It is not surprising that these ideas are at the forefront of our thinking, as they are often components of newspaper headlines or news programs on TV. Ethnic cleansing, race riots, and other aberrations often taint the topic, making it an uncomfortable discussion at best. Racial and ethnic identity is an important topic for any school to consider, whether that school is homogeneous or heterogeneous. Validating the races and ethnicities that make up the student body, faculty, and community is crucial in establishing an open and inclusive environment in schools. Integrating issues of race and ethnicity into the curriculum, thereby making them as common topics for learning as math and science, helps students to understand the topics and to develop their own perspectives on these issues.

Lesson Preparation for the Teacher

ONE TEACHER'S REFLECTION—BEING COLORFUL

I met Maria when she took a job in my school teaching Spanish. I was thrilled to work with a native speaker of the language—with someone who could help me in my own acquisition of the language as well as a rich resource for cultural information. I was immediately drawn to her optimistic viewpoint about education and her quirky and fun style of teaching. She quickly became one of the most popular teachers in our department and I enjoyed working with her, both as a friend and as a professional colleague.

One day Maria came into my classroom with a big smile on her face. "I've been invited to participate in a conference," she said. I was happy for her, but then curious. "What conference?" I asked. I had been known in my department for going to professional conferences. Maria always refused my invitations to join me. She just couldn't be bothered or was always busy. "I'm going to serve on a panel at a conference for people of color," she explained.

I was at once confused and amused. "People of color?" I thought to myself, trying not to smile or look at all surprised. Maria was whiter than me. In terms of color, I certainly had more melanin than she did. I asked her to explain a bit about the conference. She told me that she would be going along with two other colleagues from school—two black teachers. I didn't want to ask her why she was also going, since I didn't consider her a "person of color." Though I didn't question her out loud, she must have sensed my confusion and she offered: "I guess being a Latina makes me more colorful!"

I remember feeling left out, slighted, and jealous, though looking back now I am ashamed by those responses. I couldn't understand why I had such a negative reaction at the time, though in retrospect, it must have had something to do with the seeming injustice of it all. Although I might not have been interested in attending the conference, I would like to have felt that I could attend. Maria, who never expressed interest in this sort of professional development before, was being asked to not only attend the conference, but to serve on a panel discussion. I felt excluded.

Looking back on this incident, I have come to a better understanding of my feelings at the time. Being excluded made me angry and sad. At the time I didn't consider the many times that people of color have been excluded from countless events, opportunities, and rights. So, for at least this one conference, the tables were turned. I can't help but think, though, that any discussions about "color," race, or ethnicity should include everyone. After all, aren't we all one color or another?

TEACHER ACTION PROJECT: SEARCHING THE MEDIA FOR COLOR

Visit a local magazine stand and purchase several magazines that are aimed at a racial or ethnic group other than your own. For example, if you are white, you might choose *Ebony*. As you browse through the magazine, take notes on elements that seem different from magazines that are geared towards your own racial/ethnic group. What do you notice as being the most surprising? The most different? The most interesting?

Pair up with a person whose ethnicity/race is represented by the magazine and share your impressions.

References and Suggested Readings

Arboleda, T. (1998). *In the shadow of race: Growing up as a multiethnic, multicultural, and "multiracial" American.* Mahwah, NJ: Lawrence Erlbaum Associates.

Banks, J. A. (2003). *Teaching strategies for ethnic studies.* Boston: Allyn & Bacon.

Carter, R., & Goodwin, A. L. (1994). Racial identity and education. In L. Darling-Hammond (Ed.), *Review of research in education* (Vol. 20, pp. 291–336). Washington, DC: American Educational Research Association.

Delpit, L. (1995). *Other people's children: Cultural conflict in the classroom.* New York: New Press.

Espinoza-Herold, M. (2003). *Issues in Latino education: Race, school culture, and the politics of academic success.* Boston: Allyn & Bacon.

Gordon, E. W. (1999). *Education and justice, A view from the back of the bus.* New York: Teachers College Press.

Hernández Sheets, R., & Hollins, E. (Eds.). (1999), *Racial and ethnic identity in school practices.* Mahwah, NJ: Lawrence Erlbaum Associates.

hooks, bell. (1995). *Killing rage, ending racism.* New York: Henry Holt.

Howard, G. R. (2006). *We can't teach what we don't know: White teachers, multiracial schools* (2nd ed.). New York: Teachers College Press.

Jones, T. G., & Fuller, M. (2003). *Teaching Hispanic children.* Boston: Allyn & Bacon.

McCarthy, C., & Crichlow, W. (Eds.). (1993). *Race, identity, and representation in education.* New York: Routledge.

Moya, P. M. L. (2002). *Learning from experience: Minority identities, multicultural struggles.* Berkeley/Los Angeles: University of California Press.

Ogbu, J. (1994). Race stratification and education in the United States: Why inequality persists. *TC Record, (96)* 2, 264–298.

Ogbu, J., & Davis, A. (2003). *Black American students in an affluent suburb: A study of academic disengagement.* Mahwah, NJ: Lawrence Erlbaum Associates.

Paley, V. G. (1989). *White teacher.* Cambridge, MA: Harvard University Press.

Pollock, M. (2004). *Colormute: Race talk dilemmas in an American school.* Princeton, NJ: Princeton University Press.

Richardson, T. R., & Johanningmeir, E. V. (2003). *Race, ethnicity, and education: What is taught in school.* Charlotte, NC: Information Age.

Shimahara, N. K., Holowinsky, I. Z., & Tomlinson-Clarke, S. (Eds.). (2001). *Ethnicity, race, and nationality in education: A global perspective.* Mahwah, NJ: Lawrence Erlbaum Associates.

Swindker Boutte, G. (Ed.). (2002). *Resounding voices: School experiences of people from diverse ethnic backgrounds.* Boston: Allyn & Bacon.

Taylor, L. S., & Whittaker, C. R. (2003). *Bridging multiple worlds: Case studies of diverse educational communities.* Boston: Allyn & Bacon.

Waters, M. C. (1990). *Ethnic options: Choosing identities in America.* Berkley: CA: University of California Press.

Watkins, W. H., Lewis, J. H., & Chou, V. (Eds.). (2001). *Race and education: The roles of history and society in educating African-American students.* Boston: Allyn & Bacon.

Weinberg, M. (1997). *Asian-American education: Historical background and current realities.* Mahwah, NJ: Lawrence Erlbaum Associates.

Wong, S. C. (1993). Promises, pitfalls and the principles of text selection in curricular diversification. In T. Perry & J. Fraser (Eds.), *Freedom's plow* (pp. 109–120). New York: Routledge.

LESSON 7
CHANGING COLORS

GRADE LEVELS

Grades K–5

CONTENT AREAS ADDRESSED

Language Arts, Mathematics, Science, Technology, Visual Arts

TOPIC

The picturebooks *Elmer*, by David McKee, and *Chameleon's Colors*, by Chisato Tashiro, deal with the topic of color and the desire to "fit in" or be different.

RATIONALE FOR USING THIS LESSON

Young students will find the message of these picturebooks accessible and the storyline and illustrations delightful and entertaining. Teachers can use the ideas expressed by the animals in the stories as a springboard for the discussion of color, race, ethnicity, and identity with elementary-age students.

BACKGROUND INFORMATION: MELANIN

Melanin is a skin pigment (substance that gives the skin its color). Dark-skinned people have more melanin than light-skinned people. Melanin also acts as a sunscreen and protects the skin from ultraviolet light. Melanin is produced by cells called melanocytes. It provides some protection again skin damage from the sun, and the melanocytes increase their production of melanin in response to sun exposure. Freckles, which occur in people of all races, are small, concentrated areas of increased melanin production.

(Definition of *melanin*. Retrieved June 12, 2007 from
http://www.medterms.com/script/main/art.asp?articlekey=4340)

GOALS/AIMS

- Students will be encouraged to appreciate, respect, and accept races and ethnicities different from their own.
- Students will improve literary skills, such as reading, writing, communication, and critical thinking.
- Students will create an art project that reflects each student's personal identity.

CONNECTIONS TO STANDARDS

- *Language Arts Writing Standard 1:* Uses general skills and strategies of the writing process.
- *Language Arts Writing Standard 4:* Gathers and uses information for research purposes.
- *Mathematics Standard 6:* Understands and applies basic and advanced concepts of statistics and data analysis.
- *Mathematics Standard 8:* Understands and applies basic and advanced properties of functions and algebra. (Understands how graphs can represent patterns.)
- *Science: Life Sciences Standard 4:* Understands the principles of heredity and related concepts. (Knows that differences exist among individuals of the same kind of plant or animal.)
- *Science: Life Sciences Standard 5:* Understands the structure and function of cells and organisms. (Knows that plants and animals have features that help them live in different environments.)
- *Technology Standard 2:* Knows the characteristics and uses of computer software programs.
- *Visual Arts Standard 1:* Understands and applies media, techniques, and processes related to the visual arts.

(Copyright 2007. Reprinted with permission from *Content Knowledge: A Compendium of Standards and Benchmarks for K-12 Education,* 4th ed. http://www.mcrel.org/standards-benchmarks/ All rights reserved.)

MATERIALS

- A copy of the picturebook *Elmer*, by David McKee
- A copy of the picturebook *Chameleon's Colors*, by Chisato Tashiro
- Art materials:
  - large, white, unlined paper
  - crayons, markers, or paints (especially skin color shades)
  - magazines for cutting out pictures
  - glue
  - scissors

ACTIVITY

1. Write the word *melanin* on the board. Explain to students that melanin is the chemical in the skin that gives it color. The more melanin in the skin, the darker the skin looks.

2. Have students look at their own hands, and then at the hand of a friend. Have them compare the colors that they see. Distribute skin color markers or crayons. Ask if they can match a crayon to their skin color.

3. Prereading: Ask students to think about what it would be like to be unhappy with the way they looked. Ask for volunteers to tell the class about a time that they were unhappy with the way they looked, or what it might feel like for someone to feel that way.

4. Tell students that they will be learning about an animal who wasn't happy with his color. Read either *Elmer* or *Chameleon's Colors* (or both) to the students, stopping along the way to discuss the pictures and the action on each page.

5. Ask students to brainstorm a list of all the reasons why the animals wanted to change color in the books. Then ask them to think about why people might want to change color or their appearance.

6. Have students create a self-portrait using paints, markers, or magazine cutouts. Ask them to think about one thing that they like the most about themselves and to include that in the artwork. Then, ask them to include one thing that they would like to change.

7. Create a student gallery and have students explain their artwork to the class.

ACTION PROJECT

Have students visit other classrooms and take a survey of students regarding the thing they like best about their appearance (i.e., their eyes, their nose, their color, their height, their weight, etc.). When they return to the classroom, help the class to analyze the data. For older students, have them create bar graphs (with a computer graphing program such as Microsoft *Excel* or with graph paper and rulers) using the information that shows the most popular responses. Create a bulletin board and display the results to the school.

REFLECTION

Did your students make any connections to race and/or ethnicity when brainstorming ideas prior to reading the books? Did they do so after reading the books? Did anything surprise you about the students' reactions to the books? If so, what? What did students most want to change about themselves? What would you most like to change about yourself?

LESSON 8

BLACK SOLDIERS IN THE CIVIL WAR

GRADE LEVELS

Grades 6–8

CONTENT AREAS ADDRESSED

Civics and Government, History, Language Arts, Life Skills, Technology, Theater

TOPIC

Through an exploration of primary documents, students will come to a greater understanding of the role of black soldiers in the U.S. Civil War and throughout history.

RATIONALE FOR USING THIS LESSON

Interacting with authentic documents can often be more powerful than reading about historical events or issues in a textbook. Students will be led to explore a primary document and analyze the ramifications of its policies in the context of the U.S. Civil War.

BACKGROUND INFORMATION: BLACKS IN THE CIVIL WAR

"Once let the black man get upon his person the brass letter, U.S., let him get an eagle on his button, and a musket on his shoulder and bullets in his pocket, there is no power on earth that can deny that he has earned the right to citizenship."

—Frederick Douglass

The issues of emancipation and military service were intertwined from the onset of the Civil War. News from Fort Sumter set off a rush by free black men to enlist in U.S. military units. They were turned away, however, because a Federal law dating from 1792 barred Negroes from bearing arms for the U.S. Army (although they had served in the American Revolution and in the War of 1812). In Boston disappointed would-be volunteers met and passed a resolution requesting that the Government modify its laws to permit their enlistment.

The Lincoln administration wrestled with the idea of authorizing the recruitment of black troops, concerned that such a move would prompt the border states to secede. When Gen. John C. Frémont in Missouri and Gen. David Hunter in South Carolina issued proclamations that emancipated slaves in their military regions and permitted them to enlist, their superiors sternly revoked their orders. By mid-1862, however, the escalating number of former slaves (contrabands), the declining number of white volunteers, and the increasingly pressing personnel needs of the Union Army pushed the Government into reconsidering the ban.

As a result, on July 17, 1862, Congress passed the Second Confiscation and Militia Act, freeing slaves who had masters in the Confederate Army. Two days later, slavery was abolished in the territories of the United States, and on July 22 President Lincoln presented the preliminary draft of the Emancipation Proclamation to his Cabinet. After the Union Army turned back Lee's first invasion of the North at Antietam, MD, and the Emancipation Proclamation was subsequently announced, black recruitment was pursued in earnest. Volunteers from South Carolina, Tennessee, and Massachusetts filled the first authorized black regiments. Recruitment was slow until black leaders such as Frederick Douglass encouraged black men to become soldiers to ensure eventual full citizenship. (Two of Douglass's own sons contributed to the war effort.) Volunteers began to respond, and in May 1863 the Government established the Bureau of Colored Troops to manage the burgeoning numbers of black soldiers.

By the end of the Civil War, roughly 179,000 black men (10% of the Union Army) served as soldiers in the U.S. Army and another 19,000 served in the Navy. Nearly 40,000 black soldiers died over the course of the war—30,000 of infection or disease. Black soldiers served in artillery and infantry and performed all noncombat support functions that sustain an army, as well. Black carpenters, chaplains, cooks, guards, laborers, nurses, scouts, spies, steamboat pilots, surgeons, and teamsters also contributed to the war cause. There were nearly 80 black commissioned officers. Black women, who could not formally join the Army, nonetheless served as nurses, spies, and scouts, the most famous being Harriet Tubman, who scouted for the 2d South Carolina Volunteers.

Because of prejudice against them, black units were not used in combat as extensively as they might have been. Nevertheless, the soldiers served with distinction in a number of battles. Black infantrymen fought gallantly at Milliken's Bend, LA; Port Hudson, LA; Petersburg, VA; and Nashville, TN. The July 1863 assault on Fort Wagner, SC, in which the 54th Regiment of Massachusetts Volunteers lost two-thirds of their officers and half of their troops, was memorably dramatized in the film *Glory*. By war's end, 16 black soldiers had been awarded the Medal of Honor for their valor.

In addition to the perils of war faced by all Civil War soldiers, black soldiers faced additional problems stemming from racial prejudice. Racial discrimination was prevalent even in the North, and discriminatory practices permeated the U.S. military. Segregated units were formed with black enlisted men and typically commanded by white officers and black noncommissioned officers. The 54th Massachusetts was commanded by Robert Shaw and the 1st South Carolina by Thomas Wentworth Higginson—both white. Black soldiers were initially paid $10 per month from which $3 was automatically deducted for clothing, resulting in a net pay of $7. In contrast, white soldiers received $13 per month from which no clothing allowance was drawn. In June 1864 Congress granted equal pay to the U.S. Colored Troops and made the action retroactive. Black soldiers received the same rations and supplies. In addition, they received comparable medical care.

The black troops, however, faced greater peril than white troops when captured by the Confederate Army. In 1863 the Confederate Congress threatened to punish severely officers of black troops and to enslave black soldiers. As a result, President Lincoln issued General Order 233, threatening reprisal on Confederate prisoners of war (POWs) for any mistreatment of black troops. Although the threat generally restrained the Confederates, black captives were typically treated more harshly than white captives. In perhaps the most heinous known example of abuse, Confederate soldiers shot to death black Union soldiers captured at the Fort Pillow, TN, engagement of 1864. Confederate General Nathan B. Forrest witnessed the massacre and did nothing to stop it.

The document featured with this [Lesson 8 Resource Page 1] is a recruiting poster directed at black men during the Civil War. It refers to efforts by the

Lincoln administration to provide equal pay for black soldiers and equal protection for black POWs. The original poster is located in the Records of the Adjutant General's Office, 1780's–1917, Record Group 94.

(From Freeman, E., Schamel, W. B., & West, J. (1992). The fight for equal rights: A recruiting poster for black soldiers in the Civil War. *Social Education*, (56)2, 118–120 [Revised and updated in 1999 by Budge Weidman.])

GOALS/AIMS

- Students will employ creative writing skills to link historical issues and events in a writing piece.
- Students will understand the role that black soldiers played in the U.S. Civil War.
- Students will explore issues of racism and discrimination in the context of U.S. domestic policies.
- Students will explore issues of slavery in the United States.

CONNECTIONS TO STANDARDS

- *National Standards for Civics and Government:*
  - Standard II.B.1—Explain how a history of slavery distinguishes American society from other societies.
  - Standard II.D.3—Evaluate, take, and defend positions on what the fundamental values and principles of American political life are and their importance to the maintenance of constitutional democracy.
- *History Standards: Era 5—Civil War and Reconstruction (1850–1877) Standard 2A:* Demonstrate understanding of how the resources of the Union and the Confederacy affected the course of the war.
- *Language Arts Writing Standard 1:* Uses general skills and strategies of the writing process.
- *Language Arts Writing Standard 4:* Gathers and uses information for research purposes.
- *Language Arts Reading Standard 7:* Uses reading skills and strategies to understand and interpret a variety of informational texts.
- *Language Arts Viewing Standard 9:* Uses viewing skills and strategies to understand and interpret visual media.
- *Life Skills—Working with others: Standard 1:* Contributes to the overall effort of a group.
- *Life Skills—Working with others: Standard 4:* Displays effective interpersonal communication skills.
- *Life Skills—Working with others: Standard 5:* Demonstrates leadership skills.
- *Technology Standard 1:* Knows the characteristics and uses of computer hardware and operating systems.
- *Technology Standard 2:* Knows the characteristics and uses of computer software programs.
- *Theatre Standard 1:* Demonstrates competency in writing scripts.
- *Theatre Standard 2:* Uses acting skills.
- *Theatre Standard 3:* Designs and produces informal and formal productions.

(Copyright 2007. Reprinted with permission from *Content Knowledge: A Compendium of Standards and Benchmarks for K-12 Education,* 4th ed. http://www.mcrel.org/standards-benchmarks/ All rights reserved.)

MATERIALS

- Lesson 8 Resource Page 1—Recruitment Poster
- Lesson 8 Resource Page 2—Written Document Analysis Worksheet

ACTIVITY

1. Make a copy of the recruiting poster for students (Lesson 8 Resource Page 1), and direct them to read the poster and answer the following questions:

   - Who do you think is the intended audience for the poster?
   - What does the government hope the audience will do?
   - What references to pay do you find in this document?
   - What references to treatment of prisoners of war do you find in this document?
   - What evidence of discrimination during the Civil War do you find in this document?
   - What evidence of government efforts to improve conditions for black soldiers do you find in this document?
   - What purpose(s) of the government is/are served by this poster?
   - How is the design of this poster different from contemporary military recruitment posters? (Show students examples of recent or current posters.)

2. After students have completed the assignment, review it and answer any questions. Then discuss more generally the contribution and status of black soldiers in the Civil War. Alternately, provide information from the background information in this lesson.

3. Based on the recruiting poster, have students fill in Lesson 8, Resource Page 2, Written Document Analysis Worksheet.

4. Creative Writing Activities: Based on information from the poster and background information, have students write one of the following:

   - A journal entry of a member of the U.S. Colored Troops
   - A letter from a U.S. Colored Troops soldier to a son who wants to enlist
   - An account of the role of black soldiers for either an abolitionist or Confederate newspaper
   - An interior monologue of the wife of a soldier in the U.S. Colored Troops reflecting on the circumstances of her family during his absence

5. Oral Reports: Share the following information with students: President Harry S. Truman's Executive Order 9981, issued in 1948, marked the transition of the black military experience from a period of segregated troops to one of integrated forces. The order provided for "equal treatment and opportunity for all persons in the armed services" and commanded the desegregation of the military "as rapidly as possible."

   Divide the class into six groups: Civil War, Indian wars, World War I, World War II, Korea and Vietnam, and Persian Gulf War. Assign each group the task of locating information about black troops engaged in these conflicts and presenting to the class the information they discover. Encourage imaginative presentations, such as reenactments, role-plays, or other style of presentation. Students should collect information online or in the library about pay, equipment, service assignments, promotion potential, treatment of black prisoners of war, and the relation of combat service to the struggle for equal rights in each instance. Each group should attempt to locate statistical information about the numbers of black soldiers in arms for their assigned conflict and the numbers of black casualties, decorations, and commissioned officers. Outstanding individual or unit contributions in engagements should be described as well.

ACTION PROJECT

1. Arrange with the school or public library to set up a reserved reading shelf on the topic of the black Civil War experience.

2. Assign students to read a copy of Robert Lowell's poem "Colonel Shaw and the Massachusetts' 54th," alternately titled, "For the Union Dead." (The poem appears in the *Norton Anthology of American Literature*.) Ask students to consider the following questions:

   - Why does Lowell say "their monument sticks like a fishbone in the city's throat"?
   - Why do you think Shaw's father wanted no monument "except the ditch, where his son's body was thrown"?
   - What is Lowell's attitude toward the "stone statues of the abstract Union Soldier"?
   - Lowell altered the inscription on the Shaw Memorial that reads, "Omnia Reliquit Servare Rem Publicam" ("He leaves all behind to serve the Republic") to his epigraph "Relinquunt Omnia Servare Rem Publicam" ("They give up everything to serve the Republic"). How is the inscription typical of attitudes in 1897, when the memorial was dedicated? How is the epigraph, written in 1960, different, and what does that say about Lowell's attitude toward these soldiers?

   The website of the National Gallery of Art (http://www.nga.gov/onlinetours/shawwel.shtm) provides valuable information about the Shaw memorial.

3. Ask for volunteers to watch the film *Glory* (Tri Star Pictures, 1989), a fictional account of the 54th Massachusetts, then the PBS "American Experience" documentary, *The 54th Colored Infantry*. (If this program is not available, you might use the segments on black units in Ken Burns's series *The Civil War*.) Students should then review *Glory* for historical accuracy.

REFLECTION

How did your students react to the recruitment poster? Did they know anything about the participation of blacks in the Civil War? How might you follow up this activity?

Lesson 8 adapted from NARA's, *Black Soldiers in the Civil War*. Used with permission.

LESSON 8 RESOURCE PAGE 1: RECRUITMENT POSTER

TO COLORED MEN!

FREEDOM,

Protection, Pay, and a Call to Military Duty!

On the 1st day of January, 1863, the President of the United States proclaimed Freedom to over THREE MILLIONS OF SLAVES. This decree is to be enforced by all the power of the Nation. On the 21st of July last he issued the following order:

PROTECTION OF COLORED TROOPS.

"WAR DEPARTMENT, ADJUTANT GENERAL'S OFFICE, }
WASHINGTON, July 21. }

"General Order, No. 233.

"The following order of the President is published for the information and government of all concerned:–

EXECUTIVE MANSION, WASHINGTON, July 30.

"'It is the duty of every Government to give protection to its citizens, of whatever class, color, or condition, and especially to those who are duly organized as soldiers in the public service. The law of nations, and the usages and customs of war, as carried on by civilized powers, permit no distinction as to color in the treatment of prisoners of war as public enemies. To sell or enslave any Captured person on account of his color, is a relapse into barbarism, and a crime against the civilization of the age.

"'The Government of the United States will give the same protection to all its soldiers, and if the enemy shall sell or enslave any one because of his color, the offense shall be punished by retaliation upon the enemy's prisoners in our possession. It is, therefore, ordered, for every soldier of the United States, killed in violation of the laws of war, a rebel soldier shall be executed; and for every one enslaved by the enemy, or sold into slavery, a rebel soldier shall be placed as bard labor on the public works, and contiuned at such labor until the other shall be released and receive the treatment due to prisoners of war.

' "ABRAHAM LINCOLN." '

' "By order of the Secretary of War.

' " E. D. TOWNSEEND, Assistant Adjutant General." '

That the President is in earnest the rebels soon began to find out, as witness the following order from his Secretary of War:

" WAR DEPARTMENT, WASHINGTON CITY, August 8, 1863.

" Six: Your letter of the 3rd last., calling the attention of this Department to the cases of Orin II. Brown, William II. Johnston. and Wm. Wilson, three colored men captured on the gunboat Isaac Smith, has received consideration. This Department has directed that three rebel prisoners of South Carolina, if there be any such in our possession, and if not, three others, be confined in close custody and held as hostages for Brown, Johnston and Wilson, and that the fact be communicated to the rebel authorities at Richmond.

"Very respectfully your obedient servant,

"EDWIN M. STANTON, Secretary of War.

"The Hon. GIDEON WELLES, Secretary of the Navy."

And retaliation will be our practice now—man for man—to the bitter end.

LETTER OF CHARLES SUMNER,

Written with reference to the Convention held at Ponghkeepslle, July 15th and 10th, 1863, to promote Colored Enllstments.

BOSTON, July 13th. 1863.

"I doubt if, in times past, our country could have expected from colored men any patriotic service. Such service is the return for protection. But now that protection has begun, the service should begin also. Nor should relative rights and duties be weighted with nleety. It is enough that our country, aroused at last to a sense of justice, seeks to enrol colored men among its defenders.

" If my counsels should reach such persons, I would say: enlist at once. Now is the day and now is the hour. Help to overcome your cruel enemies now battling against your country, and in this way you will surely overcome those other enemies hardly less cruel, here at home, who will still seek to degrade you. This is not the time to hesitate or to higgle. Do your duty to our country, and you will set an example of generous self-sacrifice which will conquer prejudice and open all hearts.

"Very faithfully yours,   "CHARLES SUMNER"

LESSON 8 RESOURCE PAGE 2: WRITTEN DOCUMENT ANALYSIS WORKSHEET

1.	TYPE OF DOCUMENT (Check one):

_____ Newspaper	_____ Map	_____ Advertisement
_____ Letter	_____ Telegram	_____ Congressional record
_____ Patent	_____ Press release	_____ Census report
_____ Memorandum	_____ Report	_____ Other

2.	UNIQUE PHYSICAL QUALITIES OF THE DOCUMENT (Check one or more):

_____ Interesting letterhead	_____ Notations
_____ Handwritten	_____ "RECEIVED" stamp
_____ Typed	_____ Other
_____ Seals	

3. DATE(S) OF DOCUMENT:

4. AUTHOR (OR CREATOR) OF THE DOCUMENT:

POSITION (TITLE):

5. FOR WHAT AUDIENCE WAS THE DOCUMENT WRITTEN?

6. DOCUMENT INFORMATION (There are many possible ways to answer A–E.)

A. List three things the author said that you think are important.

B. Why do you think this document was written?

C. What evidence in the document helps you know why it was written? Quote from the document.

D. List two things the document tells you about life in the United States at the time it was written.

E. Write a question to the author that is left unanswered by the document.

Source: Designed and developed by the Education Staff, National Archives and Records Administration, Washington, DC 20408.

LESSON 9

THE 14TH AMENDMENT AND OUR SCHOOLS

Go to the Take Action! DVD to view a video of this lesson, "The 14th Amendment and Our Schools," in action.

GRADE LEVELS

Grades 9–12

CONTENT AREAS ADDRESSED

History, Language Arts, Life Skills, Technology, Theater

TOPIC

How well are minority rights in the American public school system defended by the 14th Amendment?

RATIONALE FOR USING THIS LESSON

Students will take on a firsthand exploration of constitutional rights by exploring the 14th Amendment and applying it to their own school context.

BACKGROUND INFORMATION: THE TEXT OF THE 14TH AMENDMENT

- **Section 1.** All persons born or naturalized in the United States, and subject to the jurisdiction thereof, are citizens of the United States and of the State wherein they reside. No State shall make or enforce any law which shall abridge the privileges or immunities of citizens of the United States; nor shall any State deprive any person of life, liberty, or property, without due process of law; nor deny to any person within its jurisdiction the equal protection of the laws.

- **Section 2.** Representatives shall be apportioned among the several States according to their respective numbers, counting the whole number of persons in each State, excluding Indians not taxed. But when the right to vote at any election for the choice of electors for President and Vice President of the United States, Representatives in Congress, the Executive and Judicial officers of a State, or the members of the Legislature thereof, is denied to any of the male inhabitants of such State, being twenty-one years of age, [and] citizens of the United States, or in any way abridged, except for participation in rebellion, or other crime, the basis of representation therein shall be reduced in the proportion which the number of such male citizens shall bear to the whole number of male citizens twenty-one years of age in such State.

- **Section 3.** No person shall be a Senator or Representative in Congress, or elector of President and Vice President, or hold any office, civil or military, under the United States, or under any State, who, having previously taken an oath, as a member of

Congress, or as an officer of the United States, or as a member of any State legislature, or as an executive or judicial officer of any State, to support the Constitution of the United States, shall have engaged in insurrection or rebellion against the same, or given aid or comfort to the enemies thereof. But Congress may by a vote of two-thirds of each House, remove such disability.

- **Section 4.** The validity of the public debt of the United States, authorized by law, including debts incurred for payment of pensions and bounties for services in suppressing insurrection or rebellion, shall not be questioned. But neither the United States nor any State shall assume or pay any debt or obligation incurred in aid of insurrection or rebellion against the United States, or any claim for the loss or emancipation of any slave; but all such debts, obligations and claims shall be held illegal and void.
- **Section 5.** The Congress shall have power to enforce, by appropriate legislation, the provisions of this article.

(From the 14th Amendment to the U.S. Constitution. Retrieved June 12, 2007 from http://www.nps.gov/archive/malu/documents/amend14.htm)

GOALS/AIMS

- Students will be able to understand the content of the 14th Amendment and apply it to current events.
- Students will discuss minority rights in the United States.
- Students will read and discuss two Supreme Court cases.

CONNECTIONS TO STANDARDS

- *History Standard 8:* Understands the institutions and practices of government created during the Revolution and how these elements were revised between 1787 and 1815 to create the foundation of the American political system based on the U.S. Constitution and the Bill of Rights.
- *Historical Understanding Standard 1:* Understands and knows how to analyze chronological relationships and patterns.
- *Language Arts Standard 7:* Uses reading skills and strategies to understand and interpret a variety of informational texts.
- *Life Skills Standards—Working with others: Standard 1:* Contributes to the overall effort of a group.
- *Life Skills Standards—Working with others: Standard 4:* Displays effective interpersonal communication skills.
- *Life Skills Standards—Working with others: Standard 5:* Demonstrates leadership skills.
- *Technology Standard 1:* Knows the characteristics and uses of computer hardware and operating systems.
- *Technology Standard 2:* Knows the characteristics and uses of computer software programs.
- *Theater: Standard 1:* Demonstrates competence in writing scripts.
- *Theater: Standard 2:* Uses acting skills.
- *Theater Standard 3:* Designs and produces informal and formal productions.

(Copyright 2007. Reprinted with permission from *Content Knowledge: A Compendium of Standards and Benchmarks for K-12 Education,* 4th ed. http://www.mcrel.org/standards-benchmarks/ All rights reserved.)

- Copy of the 14th Amendment (see Background Information)
- Copy of the Supreme Court case, "Demetrio Rodriguez v. San Antonio CSD" (1973) [available online: http//fcis.oise.utoronto.ca/~daniel_schugurensky/assignment1/1973elizondo.html]
- Copy of the Supreme Court case, "Plyer v. Doe" (1982) [available at the ACLU Montana website, "Your Constitutional Rights: 50 Pivotal U.S. Supreme Court Cases": http://www.aclumontana.org/PublicEducation/CD/50Cases/Plyler.html]

ACTIVITY

1. Have students read the 14th Amendment. Ask them to brainstorm what this Amendment means to them. Create a chart similar to the one shown in Figure 3.1 and fill in the boxes with students' ideas.

Figure 3.1   14th Amendment brainstorm chart.

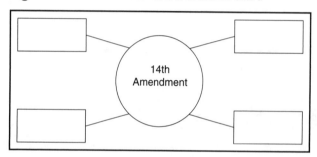

2. Ask students to read the two Supreme Court cases, either online or using printed copies. Have them summarize the main points.

3. Walk students through the details of the first case. Each student should have a copy of the text of the arguments or of a summary, such as Peter Irons's *The Courage of their Convictions* (Penguin Press, 1990).

    Summary: "Demetrio Rodriguez v. San Antonio CSD" (1973): Demetrio Rodriguez, parent of children in an underfunded school district (Edgewood) organizes a coalition of parents to challenge the system of school funding based on the 14th Amendment."

4. Ask students to think about/discuss these questions:
    - Is it fair that school districts get funding through property taxes?
    - What are some of the potential problems with this system of funding schools?

5. Walk students through the details of the second case.

    Summary: "Texas tries to charge tuition from immigrant students, the state's action is challenged based on the 14th Amendment."

6. Check for comprehension by having students break into four small groups to conduct a reenactment of the two Supreme Court cases they read. Have students represent plaintiffs and defendants and encourage them to include the main points that were argued in each case. You can serve as the judge and students from other classes might serve as witnesses or a jury.

7. After the reenactment, ask students to think about/discuss these questions:
    - Is there any case in which students in good standing should be excluded from schools?
    - Do immigrant students have a right to attend public school?

8. Class discussion: How well are minority and immigrant rights protected by the 14th Amendment? How can we improve school policy?

ACTION PROJECT

Have students investigate the funding of their own school. Have them create a proposal for their idea of the most equitable way to fund public schools. Ask students to write a letter to their local and state representatives to express their opinions on the funding for public schools in their area.

REFLECTION

What issues did students raise after reading the two Supreme Court cases? Did any of your students' comments surprise you? If so, which ones? Do you agree with school choice? Why or why not? How do you feel about schools being funded by property taxes?

Lesson 9 adapted from Cara Fenner's, *The 14th Amendment adn Our Schools*. Used with permission.

CHAPTER 4

ABILITIES AND (DIS)ABILITIES

Tell me and I forget. Show me and I remember.
Involve me and I understand.

Some Background

 Under the requirements of federal law, more students with disabilities are being included in regular classrooms than ever before. In 1975, Congress passed Public Law 94–142, the Education for All Handicapped Children Act (EHA), which attempted to correct the failure of schools to provide an adequate education for students with disabilities. In doing this, Congress rejected isolating these students in separate classrooms in favor of integrating them with students without disabilities in regular classes.

Now called the Individuals with Disabilities Education Act (IDEA), this federal law is updated roughly every five years, most recently in 2004. IDEA requires an appropriate public education for children and young adults with disabilities aged 3–21. The law does not demand that all students with disabilities be put into regular classrooms, but rather that students be placed, on a case-by-case basis, in the "least restrictive environment appropriate."

Under federal law, schools have an obligation to provide individualized help for students with disabilities so that they experience success in regular classrooms. This help might include aides, special equipment, and modified lessons and classwork as well as the services of psychologists or other professionals. But if instruction in a regular classroom, even with this help, does not benefit a student with a disability, the student may still be placed in a more restricted setting. This could be a combination of regular classes and a special education class, a special class alone, a special school, home instruction, or even a hospital or some other institution—whichever educational setting works best and is the least restrictive for the student.

Although an important reason for placing students with disabilities in regular classrooms is to maximize their academic achievement, this is not the only purpose. Many of these students benefit greatly by learning language, appropriate behavior, and other social skills from their classmates. This helps to prepare students with disabilities for the real world later in life. These social experiences in a regular classroom cannot be duplicated in a special education class or separate school settings.

Making Inclusion Work

Is inclusion in regular classrooms working? Researchers are just beginning to report results of studies comparing the achievement of students with disabilities in inclusive regular classes with those in separate special education settings. So far, the students in the inclusive classes seem to be doing a little better, particularly in social skills areas.

The early studies also indicate that the nondisabled students do not suffer academically because of the special attention given students with disabilities in their classes. In fact, there are potential benefits for nondisabled children, such as reducing their fear of others who are very different from themselves.

One of the biggest issues concerning inclusion is how to make it work well. Teachers in the mainstream classroom hold the key to success for students with special needs. Training and ongoing support in modifying curriculum and differentiated instruction are crucial to the success of inclusion. Often, by adopting nontraditional teaching methods such as cooperative learning groups, peer tutoring, learning portfolios, and oral tests, all students in the class can benefit.

Lesson Preparation for the Teacher

ONE TEACHER'S REFLECTION – I AM NOT MY DISABILITY

A few years ago I had to go to our local hospital to have some back x-rays taken. Because of some emergencies and broken equipment, I had to wait nearly two hours before I was finally taken to the x-ray room. The x-ray technician, a young woman in her early 20s, was apparently feeling rather frustrated with the delays and equipment breakdowns because she barely made eye contact with me and only mumbled a few terse words in response to my attempts to make conversation. Then, as she was positioning me for the first x-ray, another young woman stuck her head in the door and asked, "Are you about ready to go to lunch?" The x-ray tech looked at me, scrunched up her face, and replied, "Not unless you want to do this scoliosis for me." I suppose I should have said nothing, but I couldn't help myself. I looked her squarely in the eye and said, "First of all, I am not a scoliosis. I am a person who happens to have scoliosis. And secondly, believe me, you are not going to do me. You are only going to take some x-rays!" Trying to hold back her smile, the young woman in the door made a hasty getaway. The x-ray tech glared at me, but then, perhaps remembering her workshop on people-first language, looked somewhat embarrassed. Though she hardly said another word except admonishing me to hold still a couple of times as she clicked the machine, I believe she got the point. And I think my students do as well. I assume most others, like me, prefer to be thought of as people and not our medical conditions.

TEACHER ACTION PROJECT: VISITING AN INCLUSION CLASSROOM

Arrange to visit a classroom in your own or another school that follows the inclusion model. As you observe classes, keep a running log of all the techniques the teacher uses to meet the needs of students with varying abilities during the lesson. After the lesson, interview the teacher regarding the strategies used to include students with special needs. Did the teacher mention all the strategies you noted in your list? Share your list with the teacher and discuss the ways in which teaching in an inclusion classroom has changed this person's teaching.

References and Suggested Readings

Armstrong, F. (Ed.). (2000). *Disability, human rights and education: Cross-cultural perspectives.* Philadelphia, PA: Open University Press.

Bigge, J. L., Best, S. J., & Wolff Heller, K. (2001). *Teaching individuals with physical, health, or multiple disabilities.* Upper Saddle River, NJ: Pearson Education.

Biklen, D. (1992). *Schooling without labels: Parents, educators, and inclusive education.* Philadephia, PA: Temple University Press.

Block, M. E. (2000). *A teacher's guide to including students with disabilities in general physical education.* Baltimore, MD: Brookes.

Cornwall, J., & Robertson, C. (1998). *IEPs—Physical disabilities and medical conditions (Individual education plans).* London: David Fulton.

Duquette, C. (2001). *Students at risk: Solutions to classroom challenges.* Portland, ME: Stenhouse.

Gargiulo, R. M. (2005). *Special education in contemporary society: An introduction to exceptionality.* Belmont, CA: Wadsworth.

Hallahan, D., & Kauffman, J. (2001). *Exceptional learners: Introduction to special education.* Englewood Cliffs, NJ: Pearson Education.

Halvorsen, A., & Neary, T. (2000). *Building inclusive schools: Tools and strategies for success.* Boston: Allyn & Bacon.

Harwell, J. (2002). *Complete learning disabilities handbook: Ready-to-use strategies & activities for teaching students with learning disabilities.* San Francisco: Jossey-Bass.

Haskell, S. H. (1993). *The education of children with physical and neurological disabilities.* London: Nelson Thornes.

Heller, K. W., Forney, P. E., Alberto, P. A., Schwartzman, M. N., & Goeckel, T. (2000). *Meeting physical and health needs of children with disabilities: Teaching student participation and management.* Belmont, CA: Wadsworth.

Hudak, G. (1996). A suburban tale: Representation and segregation in special needs education. In J. Kincheloe, S. Steinberg, & A. Gresson (Eds.), *Measured lies: The bell curve examined.* New York: St. Martin's.

Shelton, C., & Pollingue, A. (2000). *The exceptional teacher's handbook: The first-year special education teacher's guide for success.* Thousand Oaks, CA: Corwin.

Smith, T. E. C., Polloway, E., Patton, J. R., & Dowdy, C. A., (2004). *Teaching students with special needs in inclusive settings.* Boston: Allyn & Bacon.

Stainback, W., & Stainback, S. (1996). *Controversial issues confronting special education: Divergent perspectives.* Boston: Allyn & Bacon.

Swanson, H. L. (2003). *Handbook of learning disabilities.* New York: Guilford.

LESSON 10

FDR'S SECRET

Go to the Take Action! DVD to view a video of this lesson, "Geometry and Tessellation in Islamic Art," in action.

GRADE LEVELS

Grades 3–5

CONTENT AREAS ADDRESSED

Health, History, Language Arts, Technology, Visual Arts

TOPIC

By viewing historic photos and political cartoons, students will examine the success of Franklin Delano Roosevelt's attempts to hide (or at least downplay) the extent of his physical disability. They will also learn about attitudes toward those with disabilities as they discuss the reasons for this concealment.

RATIONALE FOR USING THIS LESSON

By examining firsthand documents and photos, students can begin to understand FDR's desire to hide his disability from the world. This lesson can help foster empathy and understanding for students with physical disabilities in their own school and community.

BACKGROUND INFORMATION: FDR AND POLIO

On August 10, 1921, Franklin Delano Roosevelt was stricken with polio. While sailing that afternoon, he and his children noticed a brush fire on a small island. They went ashore and put out the fire. FDR then jogged two miles across Campobello Island for what he thought would be a refreshing swim. However, rather than feeling refreshed, he returned home totally exhausted. FDR began to read the newspaper, but felt too tired to continue. He went to bed that afternoon and never walked again.

Until his death nearly 24 years later, FDR attempted to conceal the extent of his physical disability from the American people. Was he successful? Examine the available evidence and decide for yourself.

(From Edmunt J. Sass's, *Abilities and (Dis)abilities; FDR's Secret; Speaking and Writing.*
Used with permission.)

GOALS/AIMS

- Students will understand the extent of FDR's physical disability.
- Students will determine whether FDR was successful in concealing his disability from the public.
- Students will examine some of the reasons for this concealment.

CONNECTIONS TO STANDARDS

- *Health Standard 8:* Knows essential concepts about the prevention and control of disease.
- *Historical Understanding Standard 1:* Understands and knows how to analyze chronological relationships and patterns.
- *Language Arts: Listening and Speaking Standard 8:* Uses listening and speaking strategies for different purposes.
- *Language Arts: Viewing Standard 9:* Uses viewing skills and strategies to understand and interpret visual media.
- *Life Skills: Thinking and Reasoning Standard 1:* Understands and applies the basic principles of presenting an argument.
- *Technology Standard 1:* Knows the characteristics and uses of computer hardware and operating systems.
- *Technology Standard 2:* Knows the characteristics and uses of computer software programs.
- *Visual Arts Standard 1:* Understands and applies media, techniques, and processes related to the visual arts.
- *Visual Arts Standard 4:* Understands the visual arts in relation to history and cultures.

(Copyright 2007. Reprinted with permission from *Content Knowledge: A Compendium of Standards and Benchmarks for K–12 Education*, 4th ed. http://www.mcrel.org/standards-benchmarks/ All rights reserved.)

MATERIALS

- A collection of photographs and cartoons of FDR during his presidential years. These can be accessed online from the following websites:
  - FDR Cartoons: http://www.nisk.k12.ny.us/fdr/FDRcartoons.html
  - FDR Library & Museum: http://www.fdrlibrary.marist.edu/photos.html
- Art materials:
  - large, white, unlined paper
  - crayons, markers, or paints

ACTIVITY

1. Ask students to think about having a physical or learning disability. Ask them to brainstorm reasons that people might have for hiding a disability.

2. After sharing some background about FDR's disability, explain to the students that they are to work in groups of three or four to decide if FDR was successful or unsuccessful in hiding his disability from the American people.

3. Provide groups with cartoon and photographic images of FDR from the Internet, or give them the Web addresses and have them visit the websites themselves.

4. After talking in groups, have students choose two photos and two political cartoons that they believe provide the best evidence to support their position. Each group will present their opinion to the rest of the class.

5. *Discussion.* After the students share their thoughts, photos, and cartoons (all or nearly all will probably conclude that FDR *was* successful), ask them to describe what the photos revealed regarding *how* FDR succeeded in hiding his disability. As this discussion proceeds, share with students the following information about FDR (Gallagher, 1994):

   - During the time he was president, FDR was never lifted in public nor was he ever seen in his wheelchair.
   - When out in public, FDR always stood, steadied by an aid, was seated in an ordinary chair, or sat in the backseat of his car.

- The bottoms of FDR's leg braces were painted black, so as to be difficult to distinguish from his socks and shoes, and his pants were made purposely long to cover them up.
- When he gave a speech, FDR held firmly onto a podium that was bolted to the stage. He was always seated as close to the podium as possible, and he would "walk" to the podium, with help, often from his son Elliott, by tightly gripping his son's arm.
- In his right arm Roosevelt held a cane. With this help, he could "walk," although in a curious toddling manner, hitching up first one leg with the aid of the muscles along the side of his trunk, then placing his weight upon that leg, then using the muscles along his other side, and hitching the other leg forward—first one side and then the other.

6. Ask students to think about why Roosevelt went to so much trouble to hide his disability. Though they will probably know that a "cripple" could not have been elected president, explain that in the 1920s, 1930s, and 1940s, those with disabilities "were viewed as flawed in moral character as well as body" (Gallagher, 1994, p. 30). Therefore, they "were kept at home, out of sight, in back bedrooms by families who felt a mixture of embarrassment and shame about their presence" (Longmore, 1978, p. 359).

7. Follow this discussion by asking if students believe that attitudes such as these still exist today.

8. Finally, ask students if they think that it would be possible for a person who uses a wheelchair to be elected president today. Form a debate, with teams of students presenting arguments for and against a person who uses a wheelchair, regardless of ability, in the White House. Have students use a chart such as the one in Figure 4.1 to organize their thoughts for the debate:

Figure 4.1 (Dis)ability Chart.

Candidate: Mr. Harry Garcia, wounded in fighting in the armed services. Uses a wheelchair for mobility. He has 15 years' experience as a governor and 7 as a senator.	
Reasons in favor of candidate	Reasons opposed to candidate

References

Gallagher, H. G. (1994). *FDR's splendid deception*. Arlington, VA: Vandemere.

Longmore, P. K. (1978). Uncovering the hidden history of people with disabilities. *Reviews in American History, 15*(3), 355–364.

ACTION PROJECT

Have each student choose an FDR cartoon and create a modified version portraying him as he really was—an incredibly able person who wore leg braces and used a wheelchair. Have students share their portraits/cartoons with the class in a classroom art gallery.

REFLECTION

How did the students react to the idea of hiding a disability? Do any students in your class try to hide a physical or learning disability? If so, why do you think they do this? How are people with disabilities treated by their peers in your school? By the teachers? How do you view students with disabilities in your school?

Lesson 10 adapted from Edmunt J. Sass's, *Abilities and (Dis)abilities; FDR's Secret; Speaking and Writing About People With Disabilities.* Used with permission.

LESSON II

SPEAKING AND WRITING ABOUT PEOPLE WITH DISABILITIES

GRADE LEVELS

Grades 6–8

CONTENT AREAS ADDRESSED

Health, Language Arts

TOPIC

People-first language is more appropriate and respectful of people with disabilities and should be used whenever possible. However, it is often difficult to change habits when they are ingrained in everyday life. In this lesson, students will examine the use of people-first language and learn reasons why it is more respectful than disability-first language.

RATIONALE FOR USING THIS LESSON

Talking about disabilities with adolescent students can be difficult. The desire to "fit in" is paramount and name-calling is also at its height during this time. By learning about the reasons for people-first language, students are more likely to be sensitive to the need for respectful language and understanding of students with disabilities in the school.

BACKGROUND INFORMATION: "CHALLENGING" DEFINITIONS

The use of *challenge* or *challenged* to refer to a disability is inaccurate, and can even be viewed as offensive. Despite this, the word has certainly caught on. A quick Google search of the term *physically challenged* will yield over 700,000 matches. Why has it caught on? It may be that the term is perceived as sounding kinder and gentler, and those without disabilities are more comfortable using words they feel are more "positive." However, according to the Harvard University Department of Physical Medicine and Rehabilitation's website, "use of challenged and other euphemisms avoid reality and rob people of dignity" (n.p.).

A *disability* is a measurable impairment or limitation that "interferes with a person's ability, for example, to walk, lift, hear, or learn. It may refer to a physical, sensory, or mental condition" (Schiefelbusch Institute, 1996, n.p.).

The word *handicap* is not a synonym for disability. Rather, a handicap is a disadvantage that occurs as a result of a disability or impairment. The degree of disadvantage (or the extent of the handicap) is often dependent on the adaptations made by both the individual and society (Department of Physical Medicine and Rehabilitation, 2000). Therefore, the extent to which a disability handicaps an individual can vary greatly. For instance, a person who uses a wheelchair would be much less "handicapped" in a building that is wheelchair accessible than one that is not.

In comparing the two definitions, *disability* seems the better choice for describing a person's condition, particularly in a usage such as "a child with a disability," which would conform to the current trend of using people-first language.

References

Department of Physical Medicine and Rehabilitation. (2000). *Concepts and definitions.* Boston: Harvard Medical School. Available from http://www.hmcnet.harvard.edu/pmr/rehabdef.html

Schiefelbusch Institute for Lifespan Studies. (1996). *Guidelines for reporting and writing about people with disabilities.* Lawrence, KS: Schiefelbush Institute. Available from http://www.lsi.ku.edu/lsi/intesnal/guidelines.html

GOALS/AIMS

- Students will define and differentiate between the words *disability* and *handicap.*
- Students will understand that *disability* is currently the preferred term to use when referring to students who receive special education.
- Students will understand that many people with disabilities find use of the word *challenge* to refer to a disability inappropriate and even offensive.
- Students will appropriately use people-first language and understand the reasons for its use.

CONNECTIONS TO STANDARDS

- *Health Standard 4:* Knows how to maintain mental and emotional health. (Knows behaviors that communicate care, consideration, and respect of self and others, including those with disabilities or handicapping conditions.)
- *Language Arts: Listening and Speaking Standard 8:* Uses listening and speaking strategies for different purposes.
- *Language Arts Writing Standard 1:* Uses general skills and strategies of the writing process.
- *Language Arts Writing Standard 4:* Gathers and uses information for research purposes.

(Copyright 2007. Reprinted with permission from *Content Knowledge: A Compendium of Standards and Benchmarks for K-12 Education,* 4th ed. http://www.mcrel.org/standards-benchmarks/ All rights reserved.)

MATERIALS

- Overhead projector (or computer with a destination monitor and Microsoft *PowerPoint*)
- Overhead transparency with the definitions of *disability* and *handicap* typed or written out (or the definitions typed into a *PowerPoint* presentation slide)
- Lesson 11 Resource Page: Language for Speaking and Writing About Disabilities Worksheet

ACTIVITY

1. *Introduction.* Write the words *disability, handicap,* and *challenge* on the board. Ask students to think about which of these terms they believe is preferable for referring to people (tell them not to respond aloud with their choice).
2. After a minute or two, ask for a show of hands regarding which term students prefer. Write the number of "votes" each term receives on the board. Now ask at least one student who chose each term to explain the reasons for their choice (many students are likely to choose *challenge* because they think it is the most "positive").

3. *Teacher presentation.* Explain to the students that *disability* has become the generally accepted term, having replaced the word *handicap* in federal laws (such as when changing the name of PL 94–142 to the Individuals with Disabilities Education Act from the Education of all Handicapped Children's Act). Ask if anyone knows why. Some students may have heard that the origin of the word *handicap* has something to do with being a beggar (i.e., having cap in hand, ready for donations). However, the word actually is derived from an English game in which money was held in one's cap (*Merriam-Webster Collegiate Dictionary*, 1999).

4. *Definitions.* Present the definitions of *handicap* and *disability* on overhead transparencies, read them aloud, and clarify any aspects of the definitions students find confusing.

5. Ask students if they know what you mean by "people-first language." If any are familiar with the term, ask them to describe its meaning. If no one is familiar with it, ask students what they think it implies based on the phrase "a child with a disability." After whatever discussion is generated by these questions, present the following information about people-first language:

   What is *people-first language?* Just as the term would imply, this language trend involves putting the person first, not the disability (e.g. a person with a disability, not a disabled person). Thus, people-first language tells us what conditions people have, not what they are (Schiefelbusch Institute, 1996). The following are other suggestions for referring to those with disabilities (Schiefelbusch Institute, 1996):

   - Avoiding generic labels (people with mental retardation is preferable to the mentally retarded)
   - Emphasizing abilities, not limitations (for instance, uses a wheelchair is preferable to confined to a wheelchair)
   - Avoiding euphemisms (such as physically challenged) which are regarded as condescending and avoid the real issues that result from a disability
   - Avoiding implying illness or suffering (had polio is preferable to is a polio victim, and has multiple sclerosis is preferable to suffers from multiple sclerosis)

6. *Discussion.* Ask students this question: "Is the use of people-first language important, or is it just another aspect of political correctness?" Students are usually in favor of people-first language. If not, ask students how many of them are nearsighted. Then ask if they would prefer being referred to as myopic or as a person who wears glasses. If they say that referring to someone as myopic has an additional implication other than one's vision, reply that referring to someone as spastic, retarded, crippled, or schizophrenic also implies more than just the meaning of the disability.

7. Have students complete the language worksheet (Lesson 11 Resource Page) in class in pairs or small groups.

References

Merriam-Webster. (1999). *Merriam-Webster's Collegiate Dictionary, Tenth Edition.* Springfield, MA: Merriam-Webster Inc. Available from http://www.m-w.com/

ACTION PROJECT

Have students collect documents and materials from school that are provided to parents, colleges, or the community, such as promotional brochures, course catalogs, or flyers for meetings. Many of these items can be found in the guidance office, front office, or district office. Students should also review online materials on the school's website. Ask students to review the materials for people-first language. Encourage them to rewrite the documents in people-first language if they do not already include it. Have students present their findings and revisions to the class, and then share them with the director, principal, or superintendent.

REFLECTION

How do students in your school talk about people with disabilities? How do the teachers refer to people with disabilities? Is the language in your curricula, textbooks, or other teacher materials people-first language? If not, in which materials do you notice the most inappropriate or hurtful language being used? What effect might this language have on new, inexperienced teachers?

Lesson 11 adapted from Edmunt J. Sass's, *Abilities and (Dis)abilities; FDR's Secret; Speaking and Writing About People With Disabilities*. Used with permission.

LESSON II RESOURCE PAGE: LANGUAGE FOR SPEAKING AND WRITING ABOUT DISABILITIES WORKSHEET

Correct each of the following sentences using the guidelines presented in class, including people-first language.

1. Her daughter is autistic.

2. The ARC is an organization that helps the mentally retarded.

3. I took a class about learning disabled children.

4. Gallaudet is a college for the deaf.

5. A learning disabilities teacher has many opportunities to help the mentally challenged.

6. I donate money to organizations that help the handicapped.

7. After suffering a spinal cord injury, he became a paraplegic and was confined to a wheelchair.

8. He is a polio victim who currently suffers from post-polio syndrome.

9. We saw a video about a schizophrenic woman.

10. She is afflicted with multiple sclerosis and is bedridden.

11. He was crippled from birth.

12. There was a blind girl in my calculus class.

LESSON 12

INCLUDING STUDENTS WITH DISABILITIES

GRADE LEVELS

Grades 9–12

CONTENT AREAS ADDRESSED

Health, Language Arts, Life Skills, Technology, World Language

TOPIC

Students will experience simulations of different physical and learning disabilities and will study brief cases of imaginary students. They will design ways in which they can help students with disabilities to succeed in the mainstream classroom.

RATIONALE FOR USING THIS LESSON

By learning about the different needs that students with disabilities face in the classroom, students can come to a deeper respect for their classmates. They can also learn strategies and techniques for overcoming difficulties and will be given the opportunity to help their fellow students in their studies.

BACKGROUND INFORMATION: EDUCATING THE CHILD WHO IS DIFFERENT

Before 1700, there was little toleration in Europe and America for anyone who was different. People who were blind, deaf, crippled, or mentally slow were often abused, condemned as incapable of improvement, or simply forgotten. But in the mid-1700s, the French Enlightenment began to spread the idea of helping the weak and disabled.

In 1817, Thomas Hopkins Gallaudet, a teacher of the deaf, opened the Connecticut Asylum for the Education and Instruction of Deaf and Dumb (speechless) Persons. This was the first school in America designed to serve a group of people with disabilities.

The Massachusetts School for Idiotic and Feeble-Minded Children, one of the first institutions set up specifically for children with mental disabilities, was established in 1850. At this time, most caregivers believed that young people with disabilities needed to live in institutions apart from their families.

The first important challenge to institutionalizing children with disabilities occurred toward the end of the 1800s. Alexander Graham Bell, the inventor of the telephone, believed that keeping the deaf together in institutions did not help them. Bell explained his views in a letter to Helen Keller, who later became famous for overcoming her complete loss of sight and hearing. "Exclusive association with one another," Bell wrote, "only aggravates the peculiarities that differentiate them from other people, whereas, it is our object by instruction, to do away with these differences, to the greatest extent possible." Bell went on to be an advocate for including children with disabilities in the public schools.

GOALS/AIMS

- Students will be able to understand different forms of physical and learning disabilities.
- Students will analyze and adapt lessons and other elements of the classroom environment for real or imaginary classmates with disabilities.

CONNECTIONS TO STANDARDS

- *Health Standard 4:* Knows how to maintain mental and emotional health. (Knows behaviors that communicate care, consideration, and respect of self and others, including those with disabilities or handicapping conditions.)
- *Language Arts: Writing Standard 1:* Uses the general skills and strategies of the writing process.
- *Language Arts: Reading Standard 5:* Uses the general skills and strategies of the reading process.
- *Language Arts: Reading Standard 7:* Uses reading skills and strategies to understand and interpret a variety of informational texts.
- *Language Arts: Viewing Standard 9:* Uses viewing skills and strategies to understand and interpret visual media.
- *Life Skills: Thinking and Reasoning Standard 5:* Applies basic troubleshooting and problem-solving techniques.
- *Technology Standard 1:* Knows the characteristics and uses of computer hardware and operating systems.
- *Technology Standard 2:* Knows the characteristics and uses of computer software programs.
- *World Language Standard 5:* Understands that different languages use different patterns to communicate and applies this knowledge to the target and native languages.

(Copyright 2007. Reprinted with permission from *Content Knowledge: A Compendium of Standards and Benchmarks for K-12 Education,* 4th ed. http://www.mcrel.org/standards-benchmarks/ All rights reserved.)

MATERIALS

- Lesson 12 Resource Page: Descriptions of Students with Disabilities
- Video: *How Difficult Can This Be? The F.A.T. City Workshop*—WETA (Available from http://www.ricklavoie.com/videos.html)
- A variety of adaptive hardware (i.e., a wheelchair, crutches, etc.) and software (i.e., voice recognition software) used in your school with students with special needs. (Note: It is helpful to contact your special education professionals to borrow and better understand the uses of these materials.)
- Blindfold
- Earplugs

ACTIVITY

1. Tell students that they will be experiencing different physical disabilities firsthand. Divide the class into pairs of students. Provide each dyad with the equipment to simulate a disability. For example:

   - Blindfold a student to simulate blindness.
   - Use earplugs to simulate deafness.
   - Have students sit in a wheelchair or use crutches to simulate paralysis or other physical disabilities.

2. Have groups take a walk around one corridor of school (preferably one with some obstacles, such as stairs). Make sure that the nondisabled partner takes special care not to let anything happen to the student who is experiencing the disability. Have students take turns so that each partner is able to experience the disability being simulated.

3. When the groups return, debrief with them about the experience. Ask the following questions:

   - How did you feel (in both roles—being disabled and helping the partner)?
   - What aspects of school gave you the most trouble?
   - How did people treat you during the experience?
   - How do your partner help you to navigate the hallway?

4. To simulate learning disabilities, show the film *F.A.T. City* to the class (you may prefer to show excerpts, depending on time). Discuss the film.

5. Form eight groups. The students in each group will make up a support team for one imaginary student with a disability in their class (described on Lesson 12 Resource Page). The job of each support team is to brainstorm ways to modify the activities, homework, projects, and tests of the class so that classmates with disabilities will be able to participate and learn as much as possible together with the other students. Students should research their case on the Internet or in the school library.

6. Have the support teams present to the class their ideas for modifying the classwork of classmates with different disabilities. Each team's presentation should include suggestions for teacher instructions, assignments, tests, and student participation that would help make the classroom a better place for their student.

ACTION PROJECT

Have students design a workshop for teachers on the issues of physical and/or learning disabilities. Using the information gleaned from the simulation activities in class, have students choose several powerful simulations to include in the workshop. Have students talk to the principal or superintendent to see if they can present the workshop during a teacher faculty meeting or staff development day. Ask students to incorporate some form of task or project for the teachers during the workshop. Teams of teachers and students might design "help plans" for students with physical and learning disabilities in the school. Encourage students to request feedback from teachers after their workshop.

REFLECTION

How were children with disabilities educated when you were a middle/high school student? How is it different today in the school where you teach? What are the different educational environments available for students with disabilities? What does the term *least restrictive environment* mean in your school? Are you in favor of the inclusion model? If so, why? If not, why not?

Lesson 12 adapted from Andrew Costly's, *Including Students with Disabilities.* Used with permission.

LESSON 12 RESOURCE PAGE: DESCRIPTIONS OF STUDENTS WITH DISABILITIES

- **Diana:** Due to cerebral palsy, Diana has great difficulty with muscular coordination and speaking clearly.

- **Jeremy:** Jeremy had a skiing accident a year ago that left him immobile below the neck. An aide moves him in a wheelchair from class to class and assists him in other ways at school.

- **Latasha:** Latasha has been totally deaf since birth. Because she cannot hear, she also has not learned to speak normally.

- **Carlos:** Carlos was blinded in an automobile accident at age 5. Today, he has a seeing-eye dog that guides him around school.

- **Maria:** Brain damage at birth left Maria with a number of learning disabilities. She has difficulty reading, writing, and concentrating for more than short periods of time.

- **John:** John has a severe disability called Down syndrome. This is an inherited condition that can cause mental retardation.

- **Lucia:** Lucia was born deaf and mute. She is fluent in Spanish sign language. She is having trouble learning to sign in English.

- **Udit:** Udit has a small motor disability that prevents him from writing or taking notes in class. He can't write his homework assignments in his notebooks.

CHAPTER 5

RELIGIOUS BELIEFS

There is only one religion, though there are a hundred versions of it.

GEORGE BERNARD SHAW

Some Background

Given the historical and political contexts connected to the concept of religious freedom in the United States, it is no wonder that the topic of religion would be an important one to consider when developing a multicultural classroom and school. Although it is forbidden to attempt to convert, persuade, or influence students with regard to religious beliefs in schools, it is acceptable to teach about religions and to provide students with understandings that make up a diversity of worldviews.

In 1995, U.S. Secretary of Education Richard Riley developed a "statement of principles addressing the extent to which religious expression and activity are permitted in our public schools" (Riley, http://www.ed.gov/Speeches/08-1995/religion.html). The statement and guidelines, entitled *Religious Expression in Public Schools*, was distributed to every superintendent in the United States and provides a useful overview of the "do's and don'ts" of religion and the public school system. Here is an excerpt of this document:

> **Student prayer and religious discussion:** The Establishment Clause of the First Amendment does not prohibit purely private religious speech by students. Students therefore have the same right to engage in individual or group prayer and religious discussion during the school day as they do to engage in other comparable activity. For example, students may read their Bibles or other scriptures, say grace before meals, and pray before tests to the same extent they may engage in comparable nondisruptive activities. Local school authorities possess substantial discretion to impose rules of order and other pedagogical restrictions on student activities, but they may not structure or administer such rules to discriminate against religious activity or speech.
>
> Generally, students may pray in a nondisruptive manner when not engaged in school activities or instruction, and subject to the rules that normally pertain in the applicable setting. Specifically, students in informal settings, such as cafeterias and hallways, may pray and discuss their religious views with each other, subject to the same rules of order as apply to other student activities and speech. Students may also speak to, and attempt to persuade, their peers about religious topics just as they do with regard to political topics. School officials, however, should intercede to stop student speech that constitutes harassment aimed at a student or a group of students.
>
> Students may also participate in before- or after-school events with religious content, such as "see you at the flag pole" gatherings, on the same terms as they may participate in other

noncurriculum activities on school premises. School officials may neither discourage nor encourage participation in such an event.

The right to engage in voluntary prayer or religious discussion free from discrimination does not include the right to have a captive audience listen, or to compel other students to participate. Teachers and school administrators should ensure that no student is in any way coerced to participate in religious activity.

Graduation prayer and baccalaureates: Under current Supreme Court decisions, school officials may not mandate or organize prayer at graduation, nor organize religious baccalaureate ceremonies. If a school generally opens its facilities to private groups, it must make its facilities available on the same terms to organizers of privately sponsored religious baccalaureate services. A school may not extend preferential treatment to baccalaureate ceremonies and may in some instances be obliged to disclaim official endorsement of such ceremonies.

Official neutrality regarding religious activity: Teachers and school administrators, when acting in those capacities, are representatives of the state and are prohibited by the establishment clause from soliciting or encouraging religious activity, and from participating in such activity with students. Teachers and administrators also are prohibited from discouraging activity because of its religious content, and from soliciting or encouraging antireligious activity.

Teaching about religion: Public schools may not provide religious instruction, but they may teach *about* religion, including the Bible or other scripture: the history of religion, comparative religion, the Bible (or other scripture)-as-literature, and the role of religion in the history of the United States and other countries all are permissible public school subjects. Similarly, it is permissible to consider religious influences on art, music, literature, and social studies. Although public schools may teach about religious holidays, including their religious aspects, and may celebrate the secular aspects of holidays, schools may not observe holidays as religious events or promote such observance by students.

Student assignments: Students may express their beliefs about religion in the form of homework, artwork, and other written and oral assignments free of discrimination based on the religious content of their submissions. Such home and classroom work should be judged by ordinary academic standards of substance and relevance, and against other legitimate pedagogical concerns identified by the school.

Religious literature: Students have a right to distribute religious literature to their schoolmates on the same terms as they are permitted to distribute other literature that is unrelated to school curriculum or activities. Schools may impose the same reasonable time, place, and manner or other constitutional restrictions on distribution of religious literature as they do on nonschool literature generally, but they may not single out religious literature for special regulation.

Religious excusals: Subject to applicable State laws, schools enjoy substantial discretion to excuse individual students from lessons that are objectionable to the student or the students' parents on religious or other conscientious grounds. However, students generally do not have a Federal right to be excused from lessons that may be inconsistent with their religious beliefs or practices. School officials may neither encourage nor discourage students from availing themselves of an excusal option.

Released time: Subject to applicable State laws, schools have the discretion to dismiss students to off-premises religious instruction, provided that schools do not encourage or discourage participation or penalize those who do not attend. Schools may not allow religious instruction by outsiders on school premises during the school day.

Teaching values: Though schools must be neutral with respect to religion, they may play an active role with respect to teaching civic values and virtue, and the moral code that holds us together as a community. The fact that some of these values are held also by religions does not make it unlawful to teach them in school.

Student garb: Schools enjoy substantial discretion in adopting policies relating to student dress and school uniforms. Students generally have no Federal right to be exempted from religiously-neutral and generally applicable school dress rules based on their religious beliefs or practices;

however, schools may not single out religious attire in general, or attire of a particular religion, for prohibition or regulation. Students may display religious messages on items of clothing to the same extent that they are permitted to display other comparable messages. Religious messages may not be singled out for suppression, but rather are subject to the same rules as generally apply to comparable messages.

(From Riley, Richard W. (1995, revised 1998). *Religious expression in public schools.* United States Department of Education. Available from http://www.ed.gov/ Speeches/08-1995/religion.html)

Despite the need for separation of church and state, religion is hardly invisible in the classroom setting. Muslim girls might come to school dressed in a *hijab* (a cloth covering the head) or a *burqa* (a cloth or veil covering the face) or fast during Ramadan. A Buddhist or Hindu student might require special vegetarian fare from the school cafeteria. A Jehova's Witness might need to be excluded from school celebrations or class parties. These are all visible representations of a faith that will cause classmates to question their meanings. Rather than avoiding such discussions, teachers can include all students in opportunities for sharing and exploring each other's—and the world's—faiths, including Atheism (the belief that there is no God) and Agnosticism (the belief that there is not sufficient evidence to know whether God exists).

By including religion and religious beliefs in the classroom, teachers can provide students with the tools with which to be accepting and respectful of differences. It can also serve to validate and support students in their own choices and religious practices. To summarize, the goals of including religion in your classroom are to

1. Encourage students toward *open-minded* and *objective* consideration of
- the diverse worldviews they may study in history, and
- the varied forms of "different believing" that they may encounter in their own life and times

2. Help students to appreciate those aspects of our American heritage that safeguard individual freedom of conscience.

(From http://www.teachingaboutreligion.org, n.d., n.p.)

Lesson Preparation for the Teacher

ONE TEACHER'S REFLECTION—GROWING UP JEWISH?

In my middle school the big question was "Are you Catholic or Jewish?" The dichotomous question was acceptable since there was scarcely a need to include any other choice based on the religious background of people in my town. For me, being Jewish meant that I lit the menorah for Chanukah and that I ate a Seder during Passover. We never went to temple as children and the first time I entered one was at a friend's bar mitzvah when I was thirteen. Yet Mom insisted that we were Jewish and Grandma stressed the importance of marrying a Jewish man, even though I was not yet at the stage where even boy-girl parties were de rigueur. Grandma and Mom spoke Yiddish when they didn't want me or my sister to understand, but I quickly figured out that kinder meant that us kids had done something worthy of secret discussions. Sometimes they spoke to me in "Yiddlish," or a strange mixture of half English, half Yiddish. I didn't (and still don't) understand, and today I wish that I had been taught the language.

All of my friends were Jewish and they all went to Hebrew school, though I did not attend this afterschool program. Tuition was too expensive, my mother explained, but this didn't alleviate my disappointment and frustration. While my friends complained that they had to practice the Hebrew alphabet, I looked longingly at their notebooks filled with strange and wonderful letters and wished that I could be in their shoes. How could they complain, I thought. Didn't they know how lucky they were?

My teenage years were the most tumultuous and confused as I began to consciously seek an identity. I became more introverted and started to read Albert Camus and Jean-Paul Sartre, looking for meanings. I became increasingly interested in religions such as Buddhism and Hinduism, a fascination that has lasted to this day. I started to write poetry and dress in black. I was confused, scared, and lonely, but school continued to be my savior, companion, and affirmer of my value as a person. I was encouraged by teachers to read philosophy and diverse religious texts. Social studies classes included references to Hinduism during units on the history and culture of the Indian subcontinent. Art classes involved us in studies of stained glass windows from famous Catholic churches. In English class, students were inspired to write poetry about their spiritual identities. I learned so much about my peers from their own sharing of writings in peer-review circles. These scholarly investigations kept me hopeful that there was light at the end of the existential tunnel in which I felt myself becoming increasingly trapped.

TEACHER ACTION PROJECT: EXPLORING A HOUSE OF WORSHIP

One excellent way for teachers to foster deeper understandings of religions and religious beliefs is to explore their own. Take a visit to a house of worship connected to a religion that is unfamiliar to you. Throughout the experience, write pre- and post-visit journal entries regarding your thoughts, fears, preconceived notions, and reflections. Following are one teacher's journal entries before and after a visit to a local mosque.

My visit to Fatih Camii Mosque

Pre-visit: Thoughts/Expectations/Concerns

- I might feel uncomfortable if not dressed properly.
- Will I know what to do?
- I might be asked why I was there.
- Would I offend anyone by taking photos and/or videotaping the Mosque? The service?

Pre-visit: Preparation

- I spoke at length with some of my Moslem students prior to the visit. Students told me that I would need to wear a headscarf. One student offered to borrow one from his sister for me to wear. I was advised to wear a long skirt and a long-sleeved shirt.
- I read some portions of a translation of the Koran that one student gave me as a gift.
- I spoke with a colleague at school who had gone to the Mosque with students who suggested that the boys enter first and ask if I could enter.

Post-visit: Reactions and Observations

- I was nervous as soon as I put on the head covering.
- As soon as I put on the head covering, my students began to treat me differently. I felt as if I was their younger sister. They were doing the leading and I was following.
- I felt as if the people at the Mosque were pleased that I had come. They greeted me warmly and invited in.
- I was allowed to take photos and film all I wanted.
- Two of my students left me to wash . . . they decided that they wanted to offer some prayers.
- One student is not a practicing Moslem and I sensed that he feels left out as a result. After the services, he asked his friend to teach him how to pray.
- When I saw the one student not participate, I felt close to him. I feel as he does: that, due to family, I can claim to be a member of a faith (Jewish), but I have no real connection to it. I want to feel connected, but have no one to teach me as my family is more culturally Jewish rather than religious.
- When the Imam started the call to prayer I had no idea what to do. I was frightened and felt like an intruder.
- My students told me to go to the back of the hall where the women pray.
- It upset me that women were sent away and made to stay behind a curtained-off wall. This reminded me of some orthodox Jewish temples where the women are segregated.
- I was amazed that my students knew what to do even though this was their first visit to this particular Mosque. They later explained that most all services are similar and that the motions are set down in the Koran.
- I was touched by being able to see my students in this religious environment. They seemed graceful, wise, and humble (in contrast to the way I often see them in the course of a school day!)
- The service was beautiful and felt slightly magical. I felt goose bumps and I almost cried at one point. I'm not sure why I felt so emotional. I think I was feeling grateful to see the service and also sad at not really being able to participate.
- The men in the mosque used prayer beads that look very much like rosary beads.
- After the prayer was over, the men all shook each other's hands.
- The warmth and kindness of the caretaker of the Mosque was overwhelming. He gave me an open invitation to return, with students or alone.

Post-visit: What I Learned About Myself

- I really enjoy putting myself into unfamiliar situations, but recently I need a "reason" or "excuse" to do it. In the past I was more prone to walk into a Hindu temple uninvited or to enter a strange neighborhood to explore. I feel more self-conscious in the past few years and I don't like feeling that way. I would like to explore more often.
- I discovered that I have a deep respect for religion and people's relationships with God. I feel envious of people who have an unquestioned faith in a higher being and who have prescribed ways of expressing their love and reverence in the form of prayers and religious traditions.

- I knew that I loved my students, but I feel a special bond now with these three students who took me into their world and who continue to invite me in.

- I don't like being separated from men, but was attracted to the nurturing that I experienced from my students. I didn't mind feeling passive and I enjoyed taking on the student/novice role. I feel like I would enjoy more experiences in which I was unsure of myself and not in control. I think it would balance out my teacher, "in-control-of-everything-at-all-times" nature nicely.

- I learn the most through direct experience. Although I had read some portions of the Koran, I learned far more about Islam from my students and the prayer service than from reading.

One can see from this writeup that the teacher explored much more than Islam and this particular Mosque. She related the visit to issues of gender, power and control, fam-

References and Suggested Readings

Beversluis, J. (2000). *Sourcebook of the world's religions: An interfaith guide to religion and spirituality.* Novato, CA: New World Library.

Delfattore, J. (2004). *The fourth R: Conflicts over religion in America's public schools.* Boston: Yale University Press.

Douglass, S. L. (2002). Teaching about religion. *Educational Leadership, (60)*2, 32–36.

Fraser. J. (1999). *Between church and state: Religion and public education in a multicultural America.* New York: St. Martin's.

Haynes, C. (1997). *Finding common ground: A First Amendment guide to religion and public education.* New York: Diane.

Kessler, R. (2000). *The soul of education: Helping students find connection, compassion, and character at school.* Alexandria, VA: Association for Supervision and Curriculum Development.

Kunzman, R. (2006). *Grappling with the good: Talking about religion and morality in public schools.* Albany, NY: State University of New York Press.

Marty, M. (2000). *Education, religion, and the common good: Advancing a distinctly American conversation about religion's role in our shared life.* San Francisco: Jossey-Bass.

National Center on Child Abuse and Neglect. (1996). *Religious exemptions to criminal child abuse and neglect,* Vol. 5, No. 36.

Nord, W. A. (1995). *Religion and American education: Rethinking a national dilemma.* Chapel Hill, NC: University of North Carolina Press.

Nord. W. A. (1998). *Taking religion seriously across the curriculum.* Alexandria, VA: Association for Supervision and Curriculum Development.

Palmer, P. (1993). *To know as we are known: A spirituality of education.* San Francisco: HarperSanFrancisco.

LESSON 13

CELEBRATING FAITH

GRADE LEVELS

Grades 2–6

CONTENT AREAS ADDRESSED

Geography, Language Arts, Life Skills, Technology, Theater, Visual Arts

TOPIC

This activity will involve students in the development of a classroom (and possibly school-wide) calendar of religious and cultural celebrations. They will also develop a video news report about their holiday to share with the class and school.

RATIONALE FOR USING THIS LESSON

Students from different cultural backgrounds celebrate different religious and cultural events and holidays. There are often occasions when students are absent from school in order to observe a religious or cultural holiday or event and classmates (and even the teacher) do not understand the significance of the event. Being sensitive to all students' celebrations is an important part of building an inclusive classroom.

BACKGROUND INFORMATION: CALENDARS OF DIVERSE WORLDVIEWS

BUDDHISM: *Wesak* celebrates the life of the historical Buddha. *Dhammacakka* celebrates the Buddha's first sermon where he taught the principles of Buddhism.

CHRISTIANITY: The main festivals celebrate the life of Jesus Christ: *Christmas*, celebrating his birth; *Easter*, marking his death and resurrection; *Ascension Day*, celebrating his return to Heaven. *Pentecost* celebrates the coming of the Holy Spirit onto the Disciples.

HINDUISM: There are many festivals, of which the main ones are: *Mahashivaratri* celebrating Shiva; *Holi*, the harvest festival in honor of love and of Krishna; *Divali*, celebrating the New Year and Rama and Sita, central figures of The Ramayana.

ISLAM: The Muslim calendar is lunar and moves 11 days earlier each year, compared with the Western solar calendar. *Ramadan* is the month of fasting; *Eid ul Fitr (Idul-Fitr)* marks the end of Ramadan and the giving of the Qur'an to Muhammad; *Eid ul Adha (Idul-Adha)* is the time of the Haj, the pilgrimage to Mecca and celebrates the obedience of the Prophet Ibrahim.

JUDAISM: *Passover* or *Pesach* celebrates the exodus of the Israelites from Egypt (the Seder meal in the home is observed); *Shavuot* marks the giving of the Law to Moses; *Rosh Hashanah* is the New Year festival; and *Yom Kippur*, the day of repentance. *Chanukah (Hanukkah)* celebrates the survival of the Jews.

SIKHISM: *Baisakhi* celebrates the foundation of the Khalsa; other major festivals include the Martyrdom of Guru Arjan *Dev*, the birthday of Guru Nanak, the founder of Sikhism; the Martyrdom of Guru Tegh Bahadur; and the birthday of Guru Gobind Singh.

TAOISM: The main festivals: Chinese New Year; *Ching Ming*, for the veneration of the dead; the Hungry Ghosts' festival for the release of the restless dead; and the Moon Festival, celebrating the harvest moon.

NONRELIGIOUS Worldview: Absent holy days (there are none), persons may engage in festivities and commemorations. For example, seasonally mark the equinoxes and solstices of the solar cycle with celebration of certain aspects of life and living and commemorate human advancements of reason over superstition and milestones in severance of church and state.

(Reprinted by permission from Teaching About Religion: www.teachingaboutreligion.org/
CompareWorldviews/festival_calendar.htm)

GOALS/AIMS

- Students will learn about and develop an understanding of diverse cultural and religious holidays and celebrations.

- Students will practice presentational language in the smaller classroom community and before a larger adult audience.

- Students will design and create a calendar for informational purposes.

CONNECTIONS TO STANDARDS

- *Geography Standard 1*: Uses maps and other geographic representations, tools, and technologies to acquire, process, and report information.
- *Language Arts Writing Standard 1*: Uses general skills and strategies of the writing process.
- *Language Arts Writing Standard 4*: Gathers and uses information for research purposes.
- *Life Skills—Working with others: Standard 1*: Contributes to the overall effort of a group.
- *Life Skills—Working with others: Standard 4*: Displays effective interpersonal communication skills.
- *Life Skills—Working with others: Standard 5*: Demonstrates leadership skills.
- *Technology Standard 6*: Understands the nature and uses of different forms of technology.
- *Theater: Standard 1*: Demonstrates competence in writing scripts.
- *Theater: Standard 2*: Uses acting skills.
- *Theater Standard 3*: Designs and produces informal and formal productions.
- *Visual Arts Standard 1*: Understands and applies media, techniques, and processes related to the visual arts.
- *Visual Arts Standard 4*: Understands the visual arts in relation to history and cultures.

(Copyright 2007. Reprinted with permission from *Content Knowledge: A Compendium of Standards and Benchmarks for K-12 Education*, 4th ed. http://www.mcrel.org/standards-benchmarks/
All rights reserved.)

MATERIALS

- Computers with Internet access or access to the library
- 10 sheets of large poster board or a bulletin board
- Video or DVD recorder
- Blank video tapes or recordable DVDs
- Large wall map of the world
- Arts and crafts materials:
  - Posterboard
  - Crayons or markers
  - Glue
  - Construction paper of many colors

ACTIVITY

1. Have students brainstorm as many holidays (religious primarily, but also cultural) that they personally celebrate as they can think of. As students think of holidays, list each one on the board.

2. Have each student choose a holiday they would like to report on and share with the class. If they can't think of a holiday, have them search online at KidProj's Multicultural Calendar (http://www.Kidlink.org/KIDPROJ/MCC/). (Note: The holiday they choose to research should be one that they have never heard of before or one that is not from their own culture.) Allow time for them to do research online or in the library.

3. Have students interview someone who celebrates the holiday they are researching. It could be a classmate, a family member, or someone in the school community. Students should ask questions such as the following:

   1. What does this holiday mean to you?
   2. How is the holiday celebrated in your home?
   3. What activities do children participate in during the holiday? Adults?
   4. Are there any special foods eaten during this holiday? Traditions? Clothing worn?

4. Allow time for students develop a video report in which they will share their information with the class. They should include at least one visual (drawing, clip art, or photograph) and some explanation of information in an oral form. They should also include the areas of the world where the holiday is celebrated.

5. Create a class calendar with the information gleaned from the reports. Post the calendar in the room each month. Ask the "expert" (student) who originally researched the holiday to report on it to the class when it comes up during the year.

ACTION PROJECT

Have students share their calendar with the school in the hopes that it will be shared in other classes, or with the school community at large. Create an $8^1/_2 \times 11$ inch version that can be photocopied and shared with the whole school, parents, and community members. Have students develop a presentation for the school administration (other teachers, principal, and/or superintendent) in which they present their video. Encourage students to think of ways to persuade the school to post, copy, and distribute the calendar and video so that other members of the community will know about the holidays that are celebrated in the school.

REFLECTION

How do students normally learn about each other's religions? Is there ever a time when discussing one's faith is inappropriate in school? If so, when? How can students learn to respect religious diversity in a school setting while still respecting the separation of church and state mandate?

Lesson 13 adapted from Jill Baron's, *Celebrating Faith*. Used with permission.

LESSON 14

GEOMETRY AND TESSELLATION IN ISLAMIC ART

Go to the Take Action! DVD to view a video of this lesson, "Geometry and Tessellation in Islamic Art," in action.

GRADE LEVELS

Grades 5–8

CONTENT AREAS ADDRESSED

Mathematics, Technology, Visual Arts

TOPIC

The circle and its center are the basis for patterns throughout Islamic art. Starting with the circle, any equilateral or regular polygon can be drawn within one or more surrounding circles by connecting points within or on the circle's perimeter. Tessellations are then created by the repeated creation of these drawings.

RATIONALE FOR USING THIS LESSON

Students will gain an understanding of how the Muslim world uses geometry and tessellation as a means of making meaning of the natural world. The resulting images are used to decorate houses of worship, homes, and community buildings in the Muslim world and can be said to reveal religious and spiritual beliefs. Students will also think about how visual images in other religions convey spiritual or religious meanings.

BACKGROUND INFORMATION: ISLAMIC BELIEFS MADE VISUAL

As students learn about the art produced by people of a different or earlier society, they discover that it tells them many things about what these people did, knew, and believed. Examining the geometric patterns that characterize so much of Islamic art can provide students with important insights into the technology, scientific knowledge, and religious beliefs of Muslims. Appreciation for a basic relationship between the art and the religion of Islam increases with familiarity. Careful observation of the illustrations here will provide an introduction to Islamic religious beliefs through its art.

Geometric motifs were popular with Muslim artists and designers in all parts of the world, at all times, and for decorating every surface, whether walls or floors, pots or lamps, book covers or textiles. As Islam spread from region to region, artists combined their penchant for geometry with pre-existing traditions, creating a new and distinctive Islamic art. This art expressed the logic and order inherent in the Islamic vision of the universe.

Although the shapes and structures are based on the geometry of Euclid and other Greek mathematicians, Islamic artists used them to create visual statements about religious ideas. One explanation of this practice was that Mohammad had warned against the worship of idols; this prohibition was understood as a commandment against representation of human or animal forms. Geometric forms were an acceptable substitute for the proscribed forms.

An even more important reason is that geometric systems and Islamic religious values, though expressed in different forms, say similar things about universal values. In Islamic art, infinitely repeating patterns represent the unchanging laws of God. Muslims are expected to observe strict rules of behavior exactly as they were originally set forth by Mohammad in the seventh century. These rules are known as the "Pillars of Faith":

1. pronouncing the creed (chanting an affirmation of the existence of one God and that God is Allah)
2. praying, in a precisely defined ritual of words and motions, five times a day
3. giving alms
4. fasting during the month of Ramadan (time varies according to lunar calendar)
5. making, during a lifetime, at least one pilgrimage to Mecca

The strict rules for construction of geometric patterns provide a visual analogy to religious rules of behavior. The geometric patterns used in Islamic art are aggressively two-dimensional. Artists did not want to represent the three-dimensional physical world. They preferred to create an art that represents an ideal, spiritual truth.

The star was the chosen motif for many Islamic decorations. In Islamic iconography the star is a regular geometric shape that symbolizes equal radiation in all directions from a central point. All regular stars are created by a division of a circle into equal parts. The center of the star is center of the circle from which it came, and its points touch the circumference of the circle. The center of a circle is an apt symbol of a religion that emphasizes one God, and symbol of the role of Mecca, the center of Islam, toward which all Muslims face in prayer. The rays of a star reach out in all directions, making the star a fitting symbol for the spread of Islam.

Artists did not seek to express themselves, but rather to create beautiful objects for everyone to enjoy. In analyzing Islamic patterns, we notice that seldom are two designs exactly alike. That is worrisome to Westerners because of the premium placed in the West on originality in evaluating an artist. Not so in Islam. There the artist sees himself as a humble servant of the community, using his skills and imagination to express awe of Allah, the one God, eternal and all-powerful.

(From Asia Society. Jane Norman. Copyright © 1998 http://www.askasia. org/teachers/essays/essay.php?no=96)

GOALS/AIMS

- Students will understand the ways in which geometry and tessellations serve to reveal religious beliefs in the Islamic world.
- Students will be able to design their own tessellations.
- Students will be able to discuss how visual imagery in other religions conveys religious or spiritual meaning.

CONNECTIONS TO STANDARDS

- *Mathematics Standard 3:* Patterns and Functions—Mathematics: Students will understand mathematics and become mathematically confident by communicating and reasoning mathematically, by applying mathematics in real-world settings, and by solving problems through the integrated study of number systems, geometry, algebra, data analysis, probability, and trigonometry.

- *Technology Standard 5:* Students will apply technological knowledge and skills to design, construct, use, and evaluate products and systems to satisfy human and environmental needs.
- *Visual Arts Standard 4:* Students will develop an understanding of the personal and cultural forces that shape artistic communication and how the arts in turn shape the diverse cultures of past and present society.

(Copyright 2007. Reprinted with permission from *Content Knowledge: A Compendium of Standards and Benchmarks for K-12 Education,* 4th ed. http://www.mcrel.org/standards-benchmarks/ All rights reserved.)

MATERIALS

- Lesson 14 Resource Page: Examples of Islamic Architecture
- Computer vector-based drawing program, such as *AppleWorks*, *CorelDraw*, Adobe *Illustrator*, or Geometer's *Sketchpad*
- One computer per student (Mac OS X or Windows XP preferred)
- Selection of photographs of Islamic art that depict geometric patterns on a variety of surfaces (i.e., buildings, ceramics, tiles, etc.)

ACTIVITY

1. Show students photos of Islamic art that depict geometric patterns (see Lesson 14 Resource Page for sample images). Ask them to describe what they see.

2. Explain to students that the patterns represent ideas and beliefs. Refer to portions of the Background Information and/or the following quote as appropriate:

    "The most important configuration of circles arises when six circles with equal radii are arranged around a seventh circle also with equal areas so that the edge of each circle on the outside is touching the edge of the inner circle as well as the ones beside it. From this configuration the three most important polygons to Islamic art: the triangle, the square and the hexagon, can be formed." (http://math.dartmouth.edu/~matc/math5.pattern/lesson5A&M.connection.html)

3. Start a drawing program. Create a single circle 3 inches in diameter. (Tip: Use the program's Object Size option to ensure that the diameter is accurate.) Duplicate the original circle twice, and arrange them as in Figure 5.1:

Figure 5.1

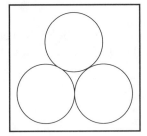

4. Connect the three centers of the circles with lines, forming an equilateral triangle (Figure 5.2).

Figure 5.2

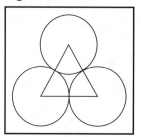

5. Select all items, and then Group them into a single object, then select Copy.

6. Paste another copy of the object onto the drawing, and move it away from the original drawing.

7. Select the new object, then Ungroup it, and select the new parts. Move each one into the desired location, as shown in Figure 5.3:

Figure 5.3

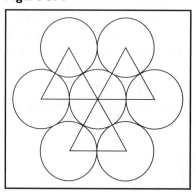

8. Continue to copy and paste the circles and triangles, as shown in Figure 5.4:

Figure 5. 4

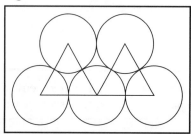

9. Highlight one triangle, then Copy and Paste it, then Flip Vertically, and fill in the remaining triangles within the circles (Figure 5.5):

Figure 5.5

10. Using the techniques described, ask students to continue to explore the creation of shapes within the constraints of a circle. Look for repeated patterns that will illustrate the concept of tessellation, as shown in Figures 5.6, 5.7, and 5.8:

Figure 5.6

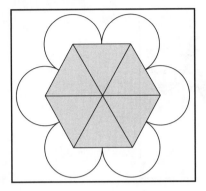

Figure 5.7

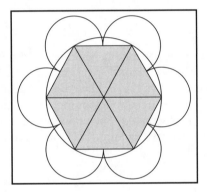

Figure 5.8

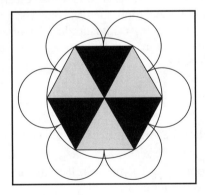

11. Extension: By coloring the various triangles or other parts of the drawing, more interesting visual designs can be achieved (Figure 5.9).

Have students share their tessellations with the class.

Figure 5.9

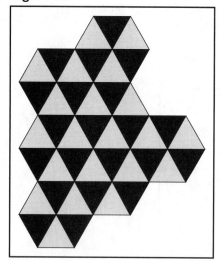

ACTION PROJECT

Have students visit a local Mosque (or take a 360-degree virtual tour of a Mosque in Singapore online at http://www.mosque.org.sg/pano/index.asp). Have students note the geometrical patterns that they can find in the architecture and decorations. If possible, ask students to interview someone at the Mosque regarding the connection between the imagery found there and how it affects worship. Encourage students to make connections to the kinds of imagery found in their own culture and/or religion and those images relate to spirituality and religious practice.

REFLECTION

How did the use of a computer program help or hinder the construction of these designs, compared to their creation by traditional tools such as compass and straight edge? Did the designs created by students indicate an understanding of tessellation? Compared to examples of Islamic art, did the creation of these drawings deepen an understanding of the underlying principles of that art?

SOURCES

The symbolism of circles in Islamic Art: http://www.salaam.co.uk/themeofthemonth/march02_index.php?l=3

Understanding the circular geometry of Islamic tessellations: http://math.dartmouth.edu/~matc/math5.pattern/lesson5A&M.connection.html

Geometry and Islam: Religious Beliefs Made Visual: http://www.askasia.org/teachers/lessons/plan.php?no=65/

El-Said, I., & Parman, A. (1976). *Geometric concepts in Islamic art*. Palo Alto, CA: Dale Seymour.

New York State Education Standards—Math, Science, Technology: http://www.emsc.nysed.gov/ciai/mst.html

Lesson 14 adapted from Frank R. Decelie, Jr.'s, *Geometry and Tessellation in Islamic Art*. Used with permission.

LESSON 15

TO PLEDGE OR NOT TO PLEDGE

GRADE LEVELS

Grades 8–12

CONTENT AREAS ADDRESSED

Language Arts, History, Theater

TOPIC

Many lawsuits have been brought against local and state governments, and even the federal government regarding the legality and constitutionality of the recitation of the Pledge of Allegiance in schools. Through a debate, students will learn about three such cases and the history of the pledge. Students will then debate the pros and cons of the inclusion of the "one nation under God" portion of the pledge.

RATIONALE FOR USING THIS LESSON

Every student knows the Pledge of Allegiance, to some degree, at least. Whether they have given thought to the recitation of the pledge or not, they will certainly understand the stories of students who have fought against being forced to do something that they believed was wrong. As adolescents have a keen sense of fairness, this lesson will awaken the middle school student's desire for justice and will inspire them to think more deeply about their own rights and responsibilities as students and citizens of the United States.

BACKGROUND INFORMATION: THE STORY OF THE PLEDGE

The original Pledge of Allegiance was written by Francis Bellamy. It was first given wide publicity through the official program of the National Public Schools Celebration of Columbus Day, which was printed in The Youth's Companion of September 8, 1892, and at the same time sent out in leaflet form to schools throughout the country. School children first recited the Pledge of Allegiance this way:

"I pledge allegiance to my Flag and to the Republic for which it stands one Nation indivisible, with Liberty and Justice for all."

"The flag of the United States" replaced the words "my Flag" in 1923 because some foreign-born people might have in mind the flag of the country of their birth instead of the United States flag. A year later, "of America" was added after "United States."

No form of the [pledge] received official recognition by Congress until June 22, 1942, when the Pledge was formally included in the U.S. Flag Code. The official name of *The Pledge of Allegiance* was adopted in 1945. The last change in language came on Flag Day 1954, when Congress passed a law, which added the words "under God" after "one nation."

Originally, the pledge was said with the right hand in the so-called "Bellamy Salute," with the right hand resting first outward from the chest, then the arm extending out from the body. Once Hitler came to power in Europe, some Americans were concerned that this position of the arm and hand resembled the Nazi or Fascist salute. In 1942 Congress also established the current practice of rendering the pledge with the right hand over the heart.

The Flag Code specifies that any future changes to the pledge would have to be with the consent of the President.

(From The Pledge of Allegiance and Our Flag of the United States: Their History and Meaning. Retrieved June 13, 2007 from http://www.wvsd.uscourts.gov/outreach/Pledge.htm)

GOALS/AIMS

- Students will be able to argue the pros and cons of reciting the Pledge of Allegiance.
- Students will develop their arguments in a debate format.
- Students will express their beliefs in a succinct and clear manner in an effort to convince the opposing side.
- Students will interpret a poem and give their opinions about its meaning.

CONNECTIONS TO STANDARDS

- *Historical Understanding Standard 1:* Understands and knows how to analyze chronological relationships and patterns.
- *Historical Understanding Standard 2:* Understands the historical perspective. Analyzes the values held by specific people who influenced history and the role their values played in influencing history.
- *United States History Standard 28:* Understands domestic policies in the post–World War II period.
- *Language Arts Standard 6:* Uses reading skills and strategies to understand and interpret a variety of literary texts.
- *Language Arts Standard 7:* Uses reading skills and strategies to understand and interpret a variety of informational texts.
- *Theater Standard 1:* Demonstrates competence in writing scripts.
- *Theater Standard 2:* Uses acting skills.
- *Theater Standard 3:* Designs and produces informal and formal productions.

(Copyright 2007. Reprinted with permission from *Content Knowledge: A Compendium of Standards and Benchmarks for K-12 Education,* 4th ed. http://www.mcrel.org/standards-benchmarks/ All rights reserved.)

MATERIALS

- Lesson 15 Resource Page 1: The Pledge of Allegiance
- Wikipedia online entry for "Pledge of Allegiance," at http://en.wikipedia.org/wiki/Pledge_of_Allegiance
- Lesson 15 Resource Page 2: Recent Court Cases Regarding the Pledge
- Lesson 15 Resource Page 3: State Information Regarding the Recitation of the Pledge of Allegiance

ACTIVITY

1. Have students read the original Pledge of Allegiance and the version we recite today (Lesson 15 Resource Page 1).

Version 1 (June 1892):

I pledge allegiance to my Flag
and the Republic for which it stands:
one Nation indivisible,
with Liberty and Justice for all.

Version 2 (June 1954):

I pledge allegiance to the Flag
of the United States of America
and to the Republic for which it stands,
one nation under God, indivisible,
with liberty and justice for all.

2. Have students brainstorm a list of the differences between the two versions. List their thoughts on the board.

3. Ask students to read and discuss the following.

President Dwight D. Eisenhower signed into law the bill authorizing adding the words "under God" to the Pledge of Allegiance on Flag Day (June 14, 1954), stating in August of that year, "These words . . . will remind Americans that despite our great physical strength we must remain humble. They will help us to keep constantly in our minds and hearts the spiritual and moral principles which alone give dignity to man, and upon which our way of life is founded" (http://en.wikipedia.org/wiki/Pledge_of_Allegiance, 2007, n.p.).

4. Read Betty Bao Lord's version of the "Pledge" to students (Note: what follows is her recital of the pledge as a free 3-year-old girl learning English in the United States after escaping from China):

I pledge a lesson to
the frog of the United
States of America.
And to the wee puppet
for witch's hands.
One Asian, in the vestibule,
with little tea and just rice for all.

From In the Year of the Boar and Jackie Robinson, by Bette Bao Lord

Ask students the following questions:

- What are your impressions of this young girl's version of the pledge?
- What portion of the pledge did this young girl omit?
- Why do you think this line/phrase was left out?
- Do you think it was done intentionally or unconsciously? Why?

5. Explain to students the concept of separation of church and state, especially as it relates to public schools. Tell students that there have been several recent court cases in which people have sued school districts and/or the government regarding the inclusion of the phrase, "One nation under God" in the pledge. Divide students into three small groups and have each group read the summaries of three recent court cases regarding the Pledge of Allegiance (Lesson 15 Resource Page 2).

6. Have one student from each group present a brief role-play, taking on the persona of the plaintiff in each case. All members of the group should help to write the script.

7. Have students highlight the arguments posed by the litigants for and against inclusion of the phrase "One nation under God" in the pledge.

8. *Class debate.* Is it acceptable to include the phrase "One nation under God" in the pledge?

ACTION PROJECT

Have students study the recitation of the Pledge of Allegiance in your school. First, have them find out the state requirements for the pledge (Lesson 15 Resource Page 3). Ask them to take a schoolwide survey regarding the pledge. If possible, have the survey sent home to parents and community members as well. Have the students analyze the results and write a class article regarding the school's attitudes towards the pledge.

REFLECTION

How do you feel about the Pledge of Allegiance? Do you feel comfortable reciting it in school? If not, why not? Do you know of anyone in your school who refuses to stand for or recite the Pledge? What might some reasons be for not standing or reciting the Pledge? How might a school allow for diversity in religious beliefs while also meeting your state's requirement (Lesson 15 Resource Page 3)?

LESSON 15 RESOURCE PAGE 1: THE PLEDGE OF ALLEGIANCE

I pledge Allegiance to the flag of the United States of America and to the Republic for which it stands, one nation under God, indivisible, with Liberty and Justice for all.

"I pledge allegiance" (I promise to be true)

"to the flag" (to the symbol of our country)

"of the United States of America" (each state that has joined to make our country)

"and to the Republic" (a republic is a country where the people choose others to make laws for them—the government is "of, by and for" the people)

"for which it stands," (the flag means the country)

"one nation" (a single country)

"under God," (the people believe in a supreme being)

"indivisible," (the country cannot be split into parts)

"with Liberty and Justice" (with freedom and fairness)

"for all." (for each person in the country . . . you and me!)

(From The Pledge of Allegiance and Our Flag of the United States: Their History and Meaning, http://www.wvsd.uscourts.gov/outreach/Pledge.htm)

LESSON 15 RESOURCE PAGE 2: RECENT COURT CASES REGARDING THE PLEDGE

Where?	California	Florida	Virginia
When?	March 2002	December 2005	August 2005
Who?	Michael Newdow– atheist, father of a school-aged girl in a public school	A 17-year-old high school junior who refused to stand during the Pledge in school	Edward Meyers, member of a Mennonite faith that opposes the mingling of church and state
What?	Claimed that his daughter was harmed by watching her teacher and classmates unfairly recite an affirmation of the existence of God every day during the Pledge.	Refused twice to stand for the Pledge in his homeroom class. Student was ridiculed and punished for not standing during the recitation of the Pledge.	Claimed that the recitation of the pledge was indoctrinating his sons with a worldview that linked God and country.
Details	Argued the unconstitutionality of the line "one nation under God" since it involved state-sponsored validation of the belief in the existence of a God.	The state of Florida requires students to stand and recite the Pledge, unless a written request is made from the parents. Plaintiff is questioning Florida law that requires written permission for exemption.	Meyers claimed that even though his sons were allowed to sit quietly during the recitation, at times substitute teachers or other school administrators would force them to participate– causing a conflict between students and the school officials.

State	School Required	School Optional	Individual Required	Individual Optional
Alabama		X		X
Alaska	X			
Arizona	X			X
Arkansas	X			X
California	X			X
Colorado[1]	X			X
Connecticut	X			X
Delaware	X			
Florida	X			
Georgia	X			X
Idaho	X			X
Illinois	X		X	
Kansas	X			
Kentucky		X		X
Louisiana		X		
Maryland	X		X	
Massachusetts	X		X	
Minnesota[2]	X			X
Mississippi[3]	X			X
Missouri	X			X
Montana	X		X	
Nevada	X			
New Hampshire	X			X
New Jersey	X		X	
New Mexico	X			
New York[4]	X			X
North Carolina		X		X
North Dakota[5]	X			
Ohio		X		
Oklahoma				X
Oregon	X			X
Pennsylvania[6]	X			X
Rhode Island	X			X
S. Carolina	X			X
South Dakota[7]		X		
Tennessee[8]	X		X	
Texas[9]	X		X	
Utah[10]	X			X
Virginia	X			
Washington	X			X
West Virginia	X			X
Wisconsin[11]	X			X

Key:

School Required	School or school district required to lead the Pledge of Allegiance
School Optional	School or district may lead the Pledge of Allegiance
Individual Required	Students required to recite the Pledge of Allegiance
Individual Optional	Students may choose not to recite the pledge (for any reason)

Note: Nearly all of the states make the pledge optional for students with religious or other objections.

Notes:

[1] Law blocked by temporary injunction August 15, 2003. Students exempt from recitation upon written request of parent/guardian.

[2] School board or charter school board of directors may waive the requirement annually by majority vote.

[3] U.S. pledge required at least once each month, as is instruction in the Mississippi pledge.

[4] Commissioner must prepare a program for state schools to use.

[5] Pertains only to students in grades 1–6.

[6] Law ruled unconstitutional July 15, 2003; parental notification required if student chooses not to participate.

[7] Statute outlines the right to display the flag, recite the Pledge of Allegiance, and sing the National Anthem in schools.

[8] Students required to recite the Pledge unless parents or legal guardians object.

[9] Students excused from reciting the Pledge upon written request of parent or guardian.

[10] Pledge required at the beginning of each day in public elementary schools. Law encourages recitation at the beginning of one day per week in public secondary schools.

[11] Pledge required at least one day per week in grades 1–8.

Source: Jennifer Piscatelli, Education Commission of the States, 2003 (http://www.ecs.org/clearinghouse/47/20/4720.htm). Reprinted by permission.

CHAPTER 6

SOCIOECONOMICS AND CLASS

The poverty of our century is unlike that of any other.
It is not, as poverty was before, the result of natural scarcity, but of a set of priorities
imposed upon the rest of the world by the rich. Consequently, the modern poor are
not pitied but written off as trash.

JOHN BERGER *(English novelist and playwright, 1926–)*

Some Background

All children in our country are entitled to a free public education, no matter their socioeconomic status or background. However, not all children receive the same quality of education. Children who attend overcrowded and underfunded city schools cannot be said to be experiencing the same quality of services in school as those who attend spacious suburban schools with high per-pupil expenditures. The curriculum might be similar, but the quality of teachers, materials, and opportunities available to students in low-income areas affect the way in which education is enacted.

Not only do the finances of a school district affect the way students learn, but also student socioeconomic status plays a significant role in leaning. Students who come to class hungry, poorly clothed, or tired cannot possibly learn as well as those who are well fed and well rested. As we understand from Maslow's *Motivation and Personality* (New York: Harper, 1954), a person's physiological needs are the most basic, and children's must be met before they can be expected to function normally in school. Children who are worried about "making ends meet" or whether their parents can pay the rent on time cannot focus on lessons or activities in the classroom.

Lesson Preparation for the Teacher

ONE TEACHER'S REFLECTION—REDUCE, REUSE, RECYCLE

Growing up in a coastal town, I remember weekends at the beach with my family. We had lively birthday parties every year, always with a creative theme, and every winter we drove down to Florida. Those trips I remember best. They were filled with fresh oranges, souvenir shops on the side of the road, and restaurant food. The days of my early childhood were secure and happy. One warm day in summer, when I was seven or eight years old, I vividly remember thinking that I must have been the luckiest girl in the world. I felt that I had everything that anyone could want, and at the time, I did.

It was during this time that I feel I learned a great deal about life and that I absorbed many of the cultural norms of the group to which my family belonged. I think that the optimism I feel today comes from this early part of my life. As I child, I thought that everyone went to Florida once a year and was surprised to hear that some of my friends didn't. I learned that men drove and women took care of travel arrangements (a stereotype which I unwittingly perpetuate even today). And since we always stayed in economy motels, I learned that cheap was best.

I learned to be creative at this early stage, as my parents, having lived through the Great Depression, were always reluctant to spend money on what they called "frivolous" things. They would not buy us many of the toys we so desperately wanted. I remember the first time I realized that I could make the things that I wanted. I was eight years old and we were visiting Disney World in Orlando. After seeing the "Bear Jamboree," I asked my mother to buy me a stuffed bear toy from the show. Mom made up some reason for not being able to buy the toy, which frustrated me, but I knew that there was no point in begging. I resigned myself to the fact that the only way for me to have that bear was to make it myself. When I got back to New York, I set to work before even unpacking. I didn't know how to sew, but it didn't matter. I made the doll from old scraps of fabric and pins, and never felt so satisfied. My sense that anything can happen if you make it happen is a direct result of the thriftiness that I was a part of for many years of my life with my family.

Once I started teaching, this resourcefulness was reborn in the classroom. While my colleagues complained about not having enough funds to buy materials for their classrooms, I fashioned banners, posters, toys, and other manipulatives from throwaway items. Cereal boxes became verb conjugation toys. Used foam core was turned onto its clean side to be remade into brand new travel posters. Garage sale finds—souvenirs from travels long since forgotten—were given a new life in my classroom display of objets d'art from around the world. I felt like the richest teacher on the planet.

However, working with kids from impoverished backgrounds provided me with greater insight into the way money—or lack of it—can influence one's worldview. Although I viewed my gently used materials as treasures, some of my poorest students looked down on them. They saw them as tattered, ugly, dirty. They told me that they came to school to get away from old things that filled their homes. They were not impressed that these items were saved from the garbage heap. Their families saved things from the trash all the time. Their kitchen tables with four unmatched chairs were salvaged from someone's garbage. Their toys and much of their clothes were hand-me-downs from older relatives. They didn't like my cereal box toys. They had their own at home.

I started looking for new materials with which to fill my classroom. I wanted to lure my students into school and make it exciting for them. Somehow I felt that if the classroom were filled with shiny new objects, they might enjoy the experience more. It reminded me of the grandeur of so many churches and cathedrals I had visited in my travels, especially in the poorest of areas. The church—with all its shiny newness and ostentatious signs of wealth—drew in the crowds in search of something better. I started to redesign my classroom as a means of drawing in crowds of kids . . . in search of something better.

TEACHER ACTION PROJECT: EXPLORING CHARITY ONLINE

Online donation websites have become increasingly popular, where teachers post a need and anyone with access to the Internet can make a contribution. Explore some of these websites and read the testimonials or case studies of several schools. What items are most teachers requesting? What types of projects have been implemented with the donations?

- Donor's Choose: http://www.donorschoose.org
- Classroom Wishlist: http://www.classroomwishlist.org
- I Love Schools: http://www.iloveschools.com
- Adopt a Classroom: http://www.adoptaclassroom.com
- Gifts in Kind: http://www.giftsinkind.org
- The Teacher's Wishlist: http://www.theteacherswishlist.com
- True Gift Donations: http://www.truegift.com

References and Suggested Readings

American Federation of Teachers. (1999). *Lost futures: The problem of child labor—A teacher's guide*. Washington, DC, Author.

Anyon, J. (1995). Race, social class, and educational reform in an inner-city school. *TC Record, 97*(1), 69–94.

Biddle, B. J. (2001). *Social class, poverty and education: Policy and practice*. London: Falmer.

Books, S. (2004). *Poverty and schooling in the U.S.: Contexts and consequences*. Mahwah, NJ: Lawrence Erlbaum Associates.

Checchi, D. (2006). *The economics of education: Human capital, family background and inequality*. Cambridge, MA: Cambridge University Press.

Duncan, G., & Brooks-Gunn, J. (Eds.). (1997). *Consequences of growing up poor*. New York: Russell Sage Foundation.

Halpern, R. (1988). Parent support and education for low-income families: Historical and current perspectives. *Children and Youth Services Review, 10*, 283–303.

Kahlenberg, R. D. (2003). *All together now: Creating middle-class schools through public school choice*. Washington, DC: Century Foundation.

Knapp, M. (1995). *Teaching for meaning in high-poverty classrooms*. New York: Teachers College Press.

Kozol, J. (1992). *Savage inequalities: Children in America's schools*. New York: Perennial.

Kozol, J. (1995). *Amazing grace: The lives of children and the conscience of a nation*. New York: Crown.

Kugler, E. G. (2002). *Debunking the middle class myth: Why diverse schools are good for all kids*. Lanham, MD: Scarecrow.

Oakes, J. (2005). *Keeping track: How schools structure inequality*, 2nd ed. New Haven, CT: Yale University Press.

Persell, C. H., & Cookson, P. W. Jr. (1985). Chartering and bartering: Elite education and social reproduction. *Social Problems, 33*(2), 114–129.

Rothstein, R. (2004). *Class and schools: Using social, economic, and educational reform to close the black-white achievement gap*. Washington, DC: Economic Policy Institute.

Shapiro, T. (2001). *Great divides: Readings in social inequality in the United States*. Mountain View, CA: Mayfield.

Sizer, T. R. (1992). *Horace's school: Redesigning the American high school*. New York: Houghton Mifflin.

Spring, J. (2003). *Educating the consumer-citizen: A history of the marriage of schools, advertising, and media*. Mahwah, NJ: Lawrence Erlbaum Associates.

LESSON 16

WE ARE ALL IN THE DUMPS WITH JACK AND GUY

Go to the Take Action! DVD to view a video of this lesson, "We Are All in the Dumps with Jack and Guy," in action.

GRADE LEVELS

Grades 3–5

CONTENT AREAS ADDRESSED

Language Arts, Life Skills, Technology, Visual Arts

TOPIC

We Are All in the Dumps with Jack and Guy, by Maurice Sendak, contains powerful illustrations and addresses serious topics such as poverty, homelessness, and child abuse. Due to the high levels of symbolism in the book, only certain aspects of the story and pictures may be accessible to elementary-level students. Teachers should first informally evaluate their students to gauge whether this is an appropriate story to include in the curriculum.

RATIONALE FOR USING THIS LESSON

In his book *The Uses of Enchantment* (New York: Knopf, 1976), Bruno Bettelheim explores the psychological role that stories play in the lives of children. He asserts that through stories, children were better able to confront their anxieties, fears, and desires in a nonthreatening way. When a parent reads aloud to a child from a storybook, the child's world and dilemmas are given credence and thus made more manageable. Bettelheim was thus a strong proponent of stories that dealt with what are traditionally considered "taboo" subjects such as death and dying or violence and forbidden desires. *We Are All in the Dumps with Jack and Guy* is a stark portrayal of homelessness, physical abuse, and other such taboo topics. Through the story, children will be able to discuss these difficult issues in a nonthreatening and even enjoyable context.

BACKGROUND INFORMATION: HOMELESS YOUTH

Definitions and Dimensions

Homeless youth are individuals under the age of eighteen who lack parental, foster, or institutional care. These young people are sometimes referred to as "unaccompanied" youth. The number of the homeless youth is estimated by the Office of Juvenile Justice and Delinquency Prevention in the U.S. Department of Justice. Their most recent study, published in 2002, reported there are an estimated 1,682,900 homeless and runaway youth. This number is equally divided among males and females, and the majority of them are between the ages of 15 and 17 (Molino, 2007). According to the U.S. Conference of Mayors, unaccompanied youth account for 3% of the urban homeless population, (U.S. Conference of Mayors, 2005). . . .

Causes

Causes of homelessness among youth fall into three inter-related categories: family problems, economic problems, and residential instability. Many homeless youth leave home after years of physical and sexual abuse, strained relationships, addiction of a family member, and parental neglect. Disruptive family conditions are the principal reason that young people leave home: in one study, more than half of the youth interviewed during shelter stays reported that their parents either told them to leave or knew they were leaving and did not care (U.S. Department of Health and Human Services (a), 1995). In another study, 46% of runaway and homeless youth had been physically abused and 17% were forced into unwanted sexual activity by a family or household member (U.S. Department of Health and Human Services (c), 1997). Some youth may become homeless when their families suffer financial crises resulting from lack of affordable housing, limited employment opportunities, insufficient wages, no medical insurance, or inadequate welfare benefits. These youth become homeless with their families, but are later separated from them by shelter, transitional housing, or child welfare policies (Shinn and Weitzman, 1996). . . .

Consequences

Homeless youth face many challenges on the streets. Few homeless youth are housed in emergency shelters as a result of lack of shelter beds for youth, shelter admission policies, and a preference for greater autonomy (Robertson, 1996). Because of their age, homeless youth have few legal means by which they can earn enough money to meet basic needs. Many homeless adolescents find that exchanging sex for food, clothing, and shelter is their only chance of survival on the streets. In turn, homeless youth are at a greater risk of contracting AIDS or HIV-related illnesses. HIV prevalence studies anonymously performed in four cities found a median HIV-positive rate of 2.3% for homeless persons under age 25 (Robertson, 1996). Other studies have found rates ranging from 5.3% in New York to 12.9% in Houston. It has been suggested that the rate of HIV prevalence for homeless youth may be as much as 2 to 10 times higher than the rates reported for other samples of adolescents in the United States (National Network for Youth, 1998).

Homeless adolescents often suffer from severe anxiety and depression, poor health and nutrition, and low self-esteem. In one study, the rates of major depression, conduct disorder, and post-traumatic stress syndrome were found to be 3 times as high among runaway youth as among youth who have not run away (Robertson, 1989). Furthermore, homeless youth face difficulties attending school because of legal guardianship requirements, residency requirements, improper records, and lack of transportation. As a result, homeless youth face severe challenges in obtaining an education and supporting themselves emotionally and financially.

(From "Homeless Youth," NCH Fact Sheet 13, National Coalition for the Homeless, August, 2007. Retrieved October 2, 2007 from http://www.nationalhomeless.org/publications/facts/youth.html)

References

Center for Law and Social Policy. (2003). *Leave no youth behind: Opportunities for congress to reach disconnected youth*. pg. 57.

National Network for Youth. (1998). *Toolkit for youth workers: Fact sheet. Runaway and homeless youth*. Washington, DC: National Network for Youth.

Robertson, M. (1989). *Homeless youth in Hollywood: Patterns of alcohol use*. Berkeley, CA: Alcohol Research Group.

Robertson, M. (1996). *Homeless youth on their own.* Berkeley, CA: Alcohol Research Group.

Shinn, M., & Weitzman, B. (1996). Homeless families are different. In *Homelessness in America.* Washington, DC: National Coalition for the Homeless.

U.S. Conference of Mayors. (2005). *A status report on hunger and homelessness in America's cities: 2005.* Washington, DC: U.S. Conference of Mayors.

U.S. Department of Health and Human Services. (1995). *Youth with runaway, throwaway, and homeless experiences . . . Prevalence, drug use, and other at-risk behaviors.* Silver Spring, MD: National Clearinghouse on Families & Youth.

U.S. Department of Health and Human Services. (1997). *National Evaluation of the runaway and homeless youth.* Silver Spring, MD: National Clearinghouse on Families & Youth.

GOALS/AIMS

- Students will be able to discuss issues of homelessness, poverty, and violence.
- Students will improve literary skills, such as reading, writing, communication, and critical thinking.
- Students will write original nursery rhymes.
- Students will use art materials to depict themes in literature.

CONNECTIONS TO STANDARDS

- *Language Arts Writing Standard 1:* Uses general skills and strategies of the writing process.
- *Language Arts Writing Standard 2:* Uses the stylistic and rhetorical aspects of writing.
- *Language Arts Writing Standard 4:* Gathers and uses information for research purposes.
- *Language Arts: Reading Standard 5:* Uses the skills and strategies of the reading process.
- *Language Arts: Reading Standard 6:* Uses reading skills and strategies to understand a variety of literary texts.
- *Life Skills Standard 4:* Displays effective interpersonal communication skills.
- *Technology Standard 1:* Knows the characteristics and uses of computer hardware and operating systems.
- *Technology Standard 2:* Knows the characteristics and uses of computer software programs.
- *Visual Arts Standard 1:* Understands and applies media, techniques, and processes related to the visual arts.
- *Visual Arts Standard 2:* Knows how to use structures (e.g., sensory qualities, organizational principles, expressive features) and functions of art.
- *Visual Arts Standard 3:* Knows a range of subject matter, symbols, and potential ideas in the visual arts.

MATERIALS

- Picturebook: Mavrice Sendak, *We Are All in the Dumps with Jack and Guy* (New York: HarperCollins, 1993).
- Art materials:
    - Large, white, unlined paper
    - Crayons, markers, or paints
    - Magazines for cutting out pictures
    - Glue
    - Scissors
    - Very large cardboard boxes (i.e., from appliances)

ACTIVITY

1. Write the word *home* on the board in a circle as the start of a brainstorming web. Have students brainstorm all the words they can think of that relate to the term *home*. Write all student suggestions into the web.

2. If the idea of homelessness does not come out of the brainstorm, talk to students about the fact that some people do not have a home, but that for them, "home" can be the street, a car, a cardboard box, or a shelter. Have students share what they know about the term *homelessness*.

3. Show students the title page of the Sendak book and ask them to describe what they see. Ask students to describe what they think the people in the scene are doing and feeling.

4. There are two nursery rhymes contained in the book. The first of which (starting, "We are all in the dumps, for diamonds are trumps") is much more stark and possibly frightening for some children. The second rhyme (starts, "Jack and Guy, went out in the rye") can also be scary, but less so than the first half of the book. Based on your knowledge of your students, read the second half of the book, or the entire book, to the students.

5. Ask students to describe what was happening in the book. The following questions can be used as prompts for discussion:

   Part One: "We are all in the dumps"

   - Describe "the dumps." Who lives there? Would you like to live there?
   - Why do you think the rats take away the little boy?
   - What do the other characters do to stop the rats?
   - What does it mean: "The houses are built without walls"?

   Part Two: "Jack and Guy"

   - Who did Jack and Guy find in the rye?
   - Why do you think the little boy had a black eye? Why do you think Jack wanted to "knock him on the head"?
   - What did Jack and Guy buy for the little boy? Why do you think it was important to buy this for him?
   - What happened to the boy at the end of the story?
   - Is this a happy story or a sad story? Why do you think so?

6. Tell students that they will be writing their own short nursery rhymes in small groups. First, show them some possible rhyming patterns:

   - AABB pattern (i.e., I saw a cat/who wore a hat/I like the duck/who drove a truck)
   - AAA pattern (i.e., Two girls run/having such fun/in the sun)
   - ABCB pattern (i.e., They went to the island/in a boat/I wanted to see them/make it float)

7. Arrange students into small groups. Have them write a short nursery rhyme (4–6 lines) about being homeless. Ask students to illustrate their poems and share them with the class.

8. Have students form small groups to build their cardboard box home. Ask each student in the team to think of three items that they can have with them in their "home." Ask them to draw or cut out of magazines the three items they can own. After each group is finished with their home, have them explain the items they chose to the class.

ACTION PROJECT

Have students visit a homeless shelter in the neighborhood. Alternately, have them take a virtual tour of the Union Rescue Mission in California online at http://www.urm.org/ (click on the link on the lower left-hand side of the page).

Have students interview the manager or director of the shelter. If doing this activity online, compose a class email letter to the director. In the letter, encourage students to find out in what ways they could help the shelter. Some possibilities:

- A sandwich-making marathon—have students sponsor a sandwich-making race and then bring the sandwiches to serve at the shelter
- A class (or grade or school) tag sale to raise money to donate to the shelter
- A coat or food drive to donate needed goods
- A tutoring service for young people at the shelter

REFLECTION

How did students react to the book? If you shared it with colleagues, supervisors, or other adults, were their reactions any different? If so, in what ways? Did you encounter any problems in sharing the book with your students? If so, what were they? How might you have presented the book differently? Would you repeat this lesson in the future? Why or why not?

LESSON 17

CLASS AND HEALTH: YOU ARE WHAT YOU EAT

GRADE LEVELS

Grades 6–8

CONTENT AREAS ADDRESSED

Economics, Health, Language Arts, Life Skills, Mathematics, Technology

TOPIC

Students learn how social class can affect nutrition and then devise a plan to help improve the nutrition of people in their communities.

RATIONALE FOR USING THIS LESSON

Most adolescents don't think too much about what they eat. They eat the lunch that is sent with them to school from home or they buy a school lunch. They know that they enjoy pizza or fast food, and vegetables tend not to be on their "top 10" list of snack items.

Students often think about what money can buy in terms of clothes they want or their favorite toys and/or games. It is unlikely that adolescents consider as often the implications that socioeconomic status has on the food they eat. This lesson will inspire teen students to think about the intersection of two issues—money and food—and will encourage them to think more critically about their relationship to both.

BACKGROUND INFORMATION: LEADING HEALTH INDICATORS

The process of selecting the Leading Health Indicators mirrored the collaborative and extensive efforts undertaken to develop Healthy People 2010. The process was led by an interagency work group within the U.S. Department of Health and Human Services. Individuals and organizations provided comments at national and regional meetings or via mail and the Internet. A report by the Institute of Medicine, National Academy of Sciences, provided several scientific models on which to support a set of indicators. Focus groups were used to ensure that the indicators are meaningful and motivating to the public.

The Leading Health Indicators will be used to measure the health of the Nation over the next 10 years. Each of the 10 Leading Health Indicators has one or more objectives from Healthy People 2010 associated with it. As a group, the Leading Health Indicators reflect the major health concerns in the United States at the beginning of the 21st century. The Leading Health Indicators were selected on the basis of their ability to motivate action, the availability of data to measure progress, and their importance as public health issues.

The Leading Health Indicators are—

- Physical Activity
- Overweight and Obesity
- Tobacco Use
- Substance Abuse
- Responsible Sexual Behavior
- Mental Health
- Injury and Violence
- Environmental Quality
- Immunization
- Access to Health Care

(From http://www.healthypeople.gov/LHI/lhiwhat.htm)

GOALS/AIMS

- Students will formulate a working definition of *social class* and explore how it might affect personal health.
- Students will gain a basic understanding of their nutritional needs.
- Students will work as a team to research, create, and present information and to further change in their communities.

CONNECTIONS TO STANDARDS

- *Economics Standard 5:* Understands unemployment, income, and income distribution in a market economy.
- *Health Education Standard 7:* Understands the relationship between the health care delivery system and the community.
- *Health Education Standard:* Uses a variety of communication skills to interact with [the community].
- *Language Arts Writing Standard 1:* Uses general skills and strategies of the writing process.
- *Language Arts Reading Standard 7:* Uses reading skills and strategies to understand and interpret a variety of informational texts.
- *Life Skills Thinking and Reasoning Standard 2:* Understands and applies basic principles of logic and reasoning.
- *Mathematics Standard 6:* Understands and applies basic and advanced concepts of statistics and data analysis.
- *Mathematics Standard 8:* Understands and applies basic and advanced properties of functions and algebra. (Understands how graphs can represent patterns.)
- *Technology Standard 1:* Knows the characteristics and uses of computer hardware and operating systems.
- *Technology Standard 2:* Knows the characteristics and uses of computer software programs.

MATERIALS

Note: This lesson requires the use of website information. Teachers whose classrooms are without student access to the Web may use printed copies of the materials.

- Computers with internet access
- Chalkboard/overhead or newsprint & markers
- Graph paper & pencils or pens
- Lesson 17 Resource Page 1: Healthy People 2010 Graphs
- Lesson 17 Resource Page 2: Leading Health Indicators

ACTIVITY

1. *Foundation.* Write the word *CLASS* in large letters on the chalkboard or on a large piece of newsprint at the front of the classroom. Be sure to leave space around the word, as this will be used in a class "webbing" activity later. Tell students that they are going to investigate the concept of social class and its impact on health issues.

2. *Task 1.* Get students thinking about the term *class* and its relationship to health issues.
   a. Briefly discuss the term. It might be helpful to begin by exploring the many meanings of the word *class* and then narrow the conversation to focus on social class. You might use examples such as, "That guy has class"; "My class was cancelled"; "He's in a different social class"; and so on. Other questions to stimulate discussion might include, Is class only defined by income? Does education affect class? How/Why? Who defines class? How might social class affect health?
   b. Explain the terms *white collar* and *blue collar* and their social class implications. Have students name some jobs that fit into each category. Ask students the following questions: How would someone use their body in these jobs? How would a lawyer or an auto mechanic use their body during the day? Would these jobs require different levels of physical exertion? How might different levels of physical exertion affect health? How might personal safety be different in each job?
   c. To further stimulate students' thoughts on this topic, have students log onto the Class in America website (http://www.pbs.org/peoplelikeus/index.html). Students should click on "STORIES" and read each story. Encourage them to think about different health-related issues that the people in the stories might encounter. (It might be good to remind students before they begin about health content areas such as stress management, disease prevention, dental hygiene, and nutrition.)
   d. Go back to the word *CLASS* on the board, and generate a "web" of class-related health issues, such as nutrition, access to medical care, amount of leisure time, stress levels, physical exertion, personal safety at work, and so on. It might help to ask some of the following questions: Who would have more leisure time—a wealthy person or a poor person? Why? (Whichever their response, ask them if the opposite might be true, too.) How could leisure time affect stress levels? How do stress levels affect health? What are some other differences in lifestyles between the upper, middle, and lower classes? Encourage them to think about differences in education, disposable income, access to medical care, and so on. How might these differences lead to different health problems? How might they change a person's approach to preventative health care?

3. *Task 2.* Students create a chart to depict how specific health issues might be affected by social class.
   a. Divide the class into groups of four (or so) and give each group a piece of graph paper. Have students write the following headings across the top: Amount of leisure time, Stress creators, Eating habits, Exercise habits, Personal safety on the job, Access to medical care. Have them write the following in a column down the left-hand side of the sheet: Migrant farm worker, Electrician, Lawyer, Company president. Ask them to note what class a person in each of the professions might belong to and why.
   b. Have students fill out the chart in groups, writing sentences to describe their thoughts. For example, they might write, "The migrant farm worker probably doesn't have a lot of leisure time because he (or she) works in the field all day. As soon as he finishes one job, he has to start the next one." They may wish to use a separate

piece of graph paper for the migrant farm worker, the electrician, the lawyer, and the company president, so they have more space to write.

   c. Groups share their lists, and classmates comment and add new information.

4. *Task 3.* Zero in on nutrition as a class issue.

   a. Discuss the importance of proper nutrition. Tell students that they are going to investigate nutritional needs and record data to use in their final project. It might be helpful to discuss the potential difficulties of maintaining a balanced diet without proper financial resources, without time, or without sufficient knowledge.

   b. Have students, individually or in groups, log on to http://www.familyfoodzone.com. This site is aimed at educating young people about nutrition. Have them click on the "Parents" link and explore the nutrition pyramid, taking notes on what they learn. These notes should cover the different vitamins and minerals they read about. They could also create a chart, listing the pyramid's different food categories down the right-hand side (milk, meat, vegetables, fruits, grains, and other) and creating three columns. In the first column they could give examples of each category (such as milk, butter, and cheese for the milk category). In the second column, they could list which nutrients each of the categories provides. In the last column they could note why those nutrients are good for you.

5. Have students research mean incomes in other nations and prepare a chart comparing mean incomes in other countries to the mean income in the United States. In a group discussion, have students brainstorm about why some countries might have a higher or lower mean income than in the United States (i.e., what factors affect the statistics). Explanations might include such factors as the high population density in certain oil-producing nations, post-colonial underdevelopment, etc.

ADAPTATION FOR OLDER STUDENTS

This lesson can be adapted for older students (9th to 11th grades) by replacing Tasks 3 and 4 with the following activity involving the Healthy People 2010 website:

1. Have students explore the Healthy People 2010 website (http://www.health.gov/healthypeople). Explain to the students that Healthy People 2010 is an initiative sponsored by the U.S. government. The U.S. Department of Health and Human Services (HHS) has developed ten-year health objectives for the nation. These are defined goals for improving the health of all Americans over the course of the next decade. Doctors and community groups around the country can look at the standards set by Healthy People 2010 and strive to reach them, just like the students might strive to get an "A" on a test.

2. Share Lesson 17 Resource Page 1: Healthy People 2010 Graphs with the students. Have the students look at the first graph, depicting the percentage of persons with fair or poor perceived health status by household income (U.S. HHS, 1995). Encourage a discussion about the components of the graph. What is it measuring? What does it indicate? What does the chart say about the connection between social class and health?

3. Next, have the students look at the second graph, depicting the relationship between education and median household income among adults 25 years and older, by gender (U.S. HHS, 1996). Ask the same questions about this graph. How is education related to social class?

4. Encourage the students to think about how each of the Leading Health Indicators (Lesson 17 Resource Page 2) might be affected by social class. Again, it might be helpful to discuss the potential difficulties of maintaining health without proper resources, without time, or without sufficient knowledge.

5. Have students discuss what the government could do to help achieve the goals set on the Healthy People 2010 website. What should the government's role be, if any? These recommendations should be shared in the letters they write in step 6.

6. Tell students that they are going to write a letter to a local political representative to inform him/her about the connection between social class and health. (Select a local

representative ahead of time.) Use the following prompt: "We have learned about class and class-related health issues. Using the CLASS web that we created, the charts, and the data gathered from the Healthy People 2010 website, write a letter explaining the connection as you see it between class, health, and at least two of the 'Leading Health Indicators' (Physical Activity Overweight and Obesity, Tobacco Use, Substance Abuse, Responsible Sexual Behavior, Mental Health, Injury and Violence, Environmental Quality, Immunization, Access to Health Care)."

EXTENSIONS

Students could explore the "What You Can Do" section on the Healthy People 2010 website (http://www.health.gov/healthypeople). Have them select a local organization that works to advance community health. As a class, the students could volunteer for the organization for a day.

ACTION PROJECT

Devise a plan to improve the nutrition of different social classes in the community. Tell students to research which programs, organizations, and institutions in their area work to improve the nutrition of different social classes. These might include food banks, soup kitchens, free lunch programs at the schools, food stamps, and so on. Have students write a paragraph about each organization or program they discover, explaining how it aims to help improve the nutrition of people in different classes. Students then choose one of the following as their action project: (1) write a letter to an elected official advocating what they believe to be the most effective or important program or (2) volunteer at a particular organization dedicated to improving nutrition.

REFLECTION

Did this activity make you think about the intersection of nutrition and socioeconomic status? If so, in what ways? How does your own socioeconomic status affect the way you eat? How does your students' status affect what they eat?

Lesson 17 adapted from Louis Alvarez's, You Are What You Eat. Used with permission.

LESSON 17 RESOURCE PAGE 1: HEALTHY PEOPLE 2010 GRAPHS

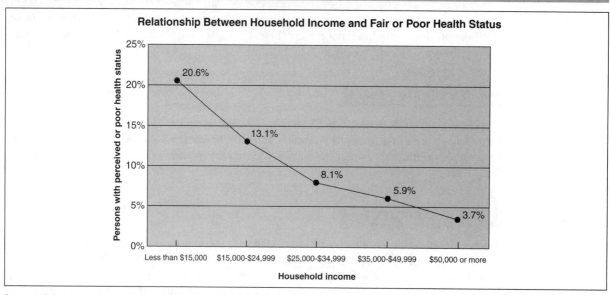

Source: U.S. Department of Commerce, Bureau of the Census. Current Population Survey. March 1997.

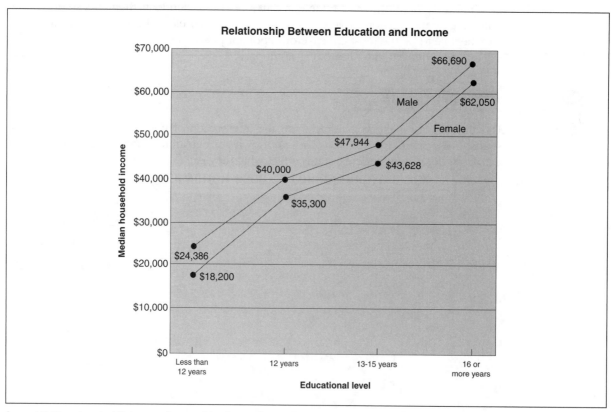

Source: U.S. Department of Commerce, Bureau of the Census. Current Population Survey. March 1997.

LESSON 17 RESOURCE PAGE 2: LEADING HEALTH INDICATORS

Leading Health Indicators

Focus Area	Physical Activity	Overweight and Obesity	Tobacco Use	Substance Abuse	Responsible Sexual Behavior	Mental Health	Injury and Violence	Environmental Quality	Immunization	Access to Health Care
Access to Quality Health Services	✓	✓	✓	✓	✓	✓	✓		✓	✓
Arthritis, Ostcoporosis, and Chronic Back Conditions	✓	✓					✓			
Cancer	✓	✓	✓	✓	✓				✓	✓
Chronic Kidney Disease	✓	✓	✓					✓		
Diabetes	✓	✓	✓						✓	✓
Disability and Secondary Conditions	✓	✓	✓	✓		✓			✓	✓
Educational and Community-Based Programs	✓	✓	✓	✓	✓	✓	✓	✓	✓	✓
Environmental Health								✓		
Family Planning				✓	✓					✓
Food Safety								✓		✓
Health Communication	✓	✓	✓	✓	✓	✓	✓	✓	✓	✓
Heart Disease and Stroke	✓	✓	✓					✓		
HIV				✓	✓	✓				✓
Immunization and Infectious Diseases									✓	✓
Injury and Violence Prevention				✓	✓		✓	✓		
Maternal, Infant, and Child Health	✓	✓	✓	✓	✓	✓	✓		✓	✓
Medical Product Safety					✓					
Mental Health and Mental Disorders				✓	✓	✓	✓			✓
Nutrition and Overweight	✓	✓	✓			✓				
Occupational Safety and Health					✓		✓	✓		
Oral Health		✓	✓	✓				✓		✓
Physical Activity and Fitness	✓	✓	✓		✓	✓		✓		
Public Health Infrastructure	✓	✓	✓	✓	✓	✓	✓	✓	✓	✓
Respiratory Diseases	✓	✓						✓		
Sexually Transmitted Diseases				✓	✓					
Substance Abuse				✓	✓	✓	✓			✓
Tobacco Use			✓					✓		✓
Vision and Hearing										✓

Source: U.S. Department of Health and Human Services. *Healthy People 2010: Understanding and Improving Health.* 2nd ed, 2000. Washington, DC: U.S. Government Printing Office.

LESSON 18

ADVERTISING AND SOCIAL CLASS

GRADE LEVELS

Grades 9–12

CONTENT AREAS ADDRESSED

Language Arts, Music, Social Studies, Technology, Visual Arts

TOPIC

Students explore how advertising helps define social class in their communities and collaborate to develop their own advertising campaigns.

RATIONALE FOR USING THIS LESSON

Young adults are subjected to advertisements in print, on television, on the Internet, and in their communities on billboards and signs. It is important for students to become aware of the aims and goals of advertisers in order to become more informed consumers. This lesson will engage students in critical thinking about advertising and inspire them to explore the intersection between advertising and socioeconomic status.

BACKGROUND INFORMATION: AWARENESS, ANALYSIS OF TOBACCO ADVERTISING MAY GO LONG WAY (BABY) TO PREVENT TEEN SMOKING

Most smokers pick up the habit as adolescents, drawn to cigarettes, in part, by advertisements featuring attractive models in playful poses, or cool movie characters whose mystique is enhanced by the fact that they smoke. Teens would be less likely to smoke by learning to view ads and other types of media more analytically, the results of a study in the current issue of *Archives of Pediatric and Adolescent Medicine* suggest.

The study provides some of the first quantitative evidence that training teens about the messages and motivations behind various types of media has the potential to reduce teen smoking. Researchers from the University of Pittsburgh School of Medicine developed a scale to measure smoking media literacy (SML), or the ability to analyze and evaluate the messages, motivations and tactics behind advertisements and other mass media portrayals of tobacco, and found that the results correlated with teens' current smoking patterns, intentions to smoke and attitudes about smoking.

Surprisingly, association between SML and smoking behaviors was stronger, in some cases, than other known predictors, such as socioeconomic status, parental smoking and stress.

"Many of the other factors that influence smoking behaviors are things that we cannot control," said Brian Primack, M.D., Ed.M., assistant professor in the school's division of general internal medicine, and lead author of the study. "Media literacy is one of the few areas in which we can actively affect change."

More than 1,200 suburban Pittsburgh high school students who participated in the study were assigned scores ranging from 0–10 based on their responses to an 18-item survey. Students responded to statements such as, "When people make movies and TV shows, every camera shot is very carefully planned," "Most movies and TV shows that show people smoking make it look more attractive than it really is," and "Advertisements usually leave out a lot of important information," by indicating whether they strongly agreed, agreed, disagreed or strongly disagreed. Higher scores represented increased SML. After controlling for 17 variables such as peer smoking, self-esteem and rebelliousness, SML still had a statistically significant association with current smoking (defined as smoking within the last 30 days), intention to smoke and general attitudes about smoking.

According to the results, a variance as small as one point on the 10-point scale corresponded with a noteworthy divergence in smoking behaviors. For instance, a student who scored a 7 was 22 percent less likely to currently be a smoker than his classmate whose SML score came in at 6, just one point lower, even after controlling for all other factors. That same student would be 31 percent less likely to be susceptible to future smoking, according to the study's results.

These findings could be particularly valuable for traditional school-based intervention programs, which tend to rely heavily on negative messages and reprimands and frequently fail in their objective to prevent teen smoking. The study suggests that such tobacco control programs could be far more effective if they incorporated SML training. Schools could also better evaluate SML educational program effectiveness by quantifying outcomes through pre- and post-training measurements.

"It's encouraging that media literacy, which is so eminently teachable, shows such promise as a component of a comprehensive tobacco intervention program," Dr. Primack said. "Our ability to measure that awareness, using the scale we developed as a tool, can provide hard evidence about which programs are effective as well."

Despite the study's promising findings, the researchers have identified several areas that warrant further examination. For example, norms—students' expressed perception of how acceptable or unacceptable smoking is among their family and friends—was the one area that showed no significant independent association with SML after controlling for all variables. The researchers plan to explore that relationship to determine if there truly is no link, or if the norm measurement tool that they used was not representative of the true nature of smoking norms. Also, the student population surveyed was homogeneous in terms of race, ethnicity and geography, so the results will need to be confirmed in more diverse populations. Finally, a longitudinal study that tracks the relationship between higher SML scores and future decisions to begin smoking could provide valuable insight.

(From "Awareness, analysis of tobacco advertising may go long way (baby) to prevent teen smoking." Retrieved June 13, 2007 from http://www.eurekalert.org/pub_releases/2006-04/uopm-aao033106.php)

GOALS/AIMS

- Students will be introduced to the concepts of *role, status,* and *social class* in America.
- Students will be able to use various criteria devised by sociologists for determining class ranking and discuss the validity and appropriateness of these criteria.

- Students will be able to discuss role, status, and social class and apply these terms to their surroundings.
- Students will practice research, questioning, discussion, and writing skills.

CONNECTIONS TO STANDARDS

- *Language Arts. Standard: 8. Level III:* Middle School/Jr. High (Grades 6–8). Level IV: High School (Grades 9–12). Demonstrates competence in speaking and listening as tools for learning.
- *Music Standard 7:* Understands the relationship between music and history and culture.
- *Social Studies (National Curriculum Standards for the Social Studies):* Topic: Social Groupings: Function and Influence on Behavior: Apply concepts such as role, status, and social class in describing the connections and interactions of individuals, groups, and institutions in society.
- *Social Studies/Behavioral Studies. Standard: 1. Level III:* Middle School/Jr. High (Grades 6–8). Level IV: High School (Grades 9–12). Understands that group and cultural influences contribute to human development, identity, and behavior.
- *Social Studies/Behavioral Studies. Standard: 2. Level III:* Middle School/Jr. High (Grades 6–8). Level IV: High School (Grades 9–12). Understands various meanings of social group, general implications of group membership, and different ways that groups function.
- *Technology Standard 1:* Knows the characteristics and uses of computer hardware and operating systems.
- *Technology Standard 2:* Knows the characteristics and uses of computer software programs.
- *Visual Arts Standard 1:* Understands and applies media, techniques, and processes related to the visual arts.
- *Visual Arts Standard 4:* Understands the visual arts in relation to history and cultures.

(Copoyright 2007. Reprinted with permission from *Content Knowledge. A Compendium of Standards and Benchmark for K-12 Education*, 4th ed. http://www.mcrel.org/standards-bechmarks/ All rights reserved.)

MATERIALS

- Internet access
- Magazines that contain a variety of pictures of houses, cars, clothing, and clothing in contemporary America
- Scissors
- Paste
- Poster board or a large classroom bulletin board

ACTIVITY

1. To introduce the lesson, cut out four "face" pictures from a magazine. The pictures should represent young and old men and women of different ethnic backgrounds. Post these pictures on the board. Ask students to guess whether each person shown is rich or poor, what kind of job they have, and what kind of house they might live in. Time permitting, make this a matching game: cut out pictures of cars, houses, clothing, and so on and ask students to match each object with a person. Students record their observations and the reasons for their choices in their journals. Be ready to introduce the concept of stereotyping as students share their observations with the class.

2. Have students play the game "Chintz or Shag," found at http://www.pbs.org/peoplelikeus/games.

3. After playing the game, divide students into small groups to discuss the outcome of the game. Were the results a surprise? Students should speculate on the criteria used in the game. What was its basis? Do they agree with the results? Why or why not? What does it mean to be "middle middle" class or "nouveau riche?" Who is the term *old money* referring to? Do the students think they can tell what class somebody is by looking at them or by looking at their living room? Where might Americans in the uppermost classes live? People in the lowest classes? To what extent is class in America defined by what individuals own? Students record their reactions in journals.

4. Students then work in small groups to prepare a list of criteria for the "middle middle" class of their community. Are people in their community judged by what cars they drive, which sports they play, or what sorts of clothes they wear? You may wish to prompt students with questions such as, What is typical behavior in the community? Is there a kind of car that most families drive? Are there certain stores that most people go to? Are there particular sports that many people play? Is there are difference between the richest people and the poorest people in our community in terms of what they own (types of cars, houses, and clothes)? Students should work together to come up with agreed criteria. You may want the class to discuss to what extent the criteria are stereotypical or determined by advertising. Have students follow up their own thoughts about class in their community by visiting Claritas at the PRIZM website (http://www.claritas.com/ MyBestSegments/Default.jsp), which allows them to type in their zip code and see data about their community. Students can have a discussion comparing their perceptions with the real data.

5. After looking at the PRIZM zip code data, encourage group discussion about how advertising companies might use this type of information to create ads that target specific audiences. For example, the site gives a list of things people in certain clusters are likely to do, such as "watch *Nightline*" or "drink Pepsi Free®." How would knowing about these consumption patterns change the marketing strategies of advertising companies? If advertisers know that a certain community is likely to "shop at T. J. Maxx" or "read *Gourmet*," how might it affect what products they market to that community, or where they put their advertisements? Encourage students to talk about how consumption patterns relate to class—are certain magazines, cars, foods, or clothes considered more upper or lower class than others? Why do they think this might be so? Do advertisements reinforce the social class status quo, change it, or have no affect at all? Can they think of examples?

6. Working in small groups, have students pick one of the clusters in their zip code, as described on the PRIZM site, and develop an ad that targets that community (the clusters have such names as "Young Literati" and "Hard Scrabble"). They should pick an item such as basketball shoes or a brand of soft drink, and plan a campaign around the product. Students may use the criteria they established in step 4 and the information the PRIZM site provides about income levels, professions, and consumption patterns as they decide what product people in their selected cluster might buy. They should also consider the PRIZM information as they decide how to pitch their product to the cluster, considering such things as the price of the merchandise, a good setting for the ad, and what language to write the advertisement in. When they finish, they should be ready to explain how they integrated the criteria established in step 4 and the PRIZM data into their plan.

7. Students share their ad/product in a "sales pitch" to the class. The presentation should include either a print ad, a radio commercial on audiotape/CD, or a TV commercial on videotape/DVD (the last two types of presentations might include music).

EXTENSION ACTIVITIES

1. Introduce the concept of *capitalism* as an economic system. Have students research the difference between a market system (as found in the United States) and a command system (as found in the former Soviet Union). Explain that the American economic system is a market system and that stimulating demand through advertising is a fundamental part of the way the American economy works. Students can further explore how forces of supply and demand in a market system answer basic economic questions such as what to produce, how to produce, and for whom to produce through a lesson found at http://ecedweb.unomaha.edu/Dem_Sup/demand.htm.

2. The issues discussed in this lesson are addressed in a slightly different but fascinating manner at http://www.pbs.org/kcts/affluenza/diag/diag.html. The site has very well-done chronology of consumption issues in Western society.

3. Check out the phone book for advertising departments of local newspapers, radio, and television stations. Invite a guest speaker to the class from one of these sources to discuss the targeting of media in your locale.

ACTION PROJECT

Have students take a look at various websites and attempt to determine what is being marketed to who and why. They might also tape TV commercials and look at the same thing, or use magazine ads. In small groups, have students design presentations (*PowerPoint*, video, or otherwise) to reveal what they have discovered. They can take their shows "on the road" to younger students in the school and educate them on how advertising helps define social class.

REFLECTION

Are there any advertisements in your school? For example, do you have any posters in the cafeteria or on book covers that students see regularly? What advertisements do your students see on their way to school in the morning (i.e., highway signs, billboards, or in shop windows)? What are the messages being sent in these advertisements? How do these ads target certain groups of students? What are some more ways in which you might educate your students about advertisements in the media?

Lesson 18 adapted from Louis Alvarez's, Class and Health: You Are What You Eat. Used with permission.

CHAPTER **7**

LANGUAGE AND COMMUNICATION

We dissect nature along lines laid down by our native language. Language is not simply a reporting device for experience but a defining framework for it.

BENJAMIN WHORF (American linguist, 1897–1941)

Some Background

Identity, culture, socioecomic status, and religion are all embedded in language. Language use at once reveals and defines who we are in relationship to others. A Boston Brahmin accent will immediately evoke one image of its speaker, while a Brooklyn accent will bring to mind a different image. We cannot escape being defined by the language we use, but students can begin to understand the complicated ways in which language reveals identity.

Not only are accents and the sound of a language indicative of elements of culture, but so are the kinds of words we use and the cadence or rhythm of our speech, as well as the facility with which we speak one language or another. Think about the ways in which you might react differently to students who speak Ebonics or stilted English, or use slang.

Language also includes such nonverbal elements as proxemics (how close people stand to each other when speaking), facial expressions, and gestures. What is appropriate in one culture or context is not necessarily acceptable in another. Communication involves coordination of all of these elements. When some elements cause negative reactions in one of the interlocutors, messages can be misperceived or even ignored. Language is *that* powerful, and it is a vital part of every minute of every day spent in school.

Lesson Preparation for the Teacher

REFLECTIONS ON LANGUAGE—TALKING GOOD

"All my teachers always made me feel stupid for speaking the way I do. But you've shown me that it's not bad and that there is a reason that I speak how I do and now I'm not embarrassed anymore. In fact, language differences really interest me and learning Spanish has helped me see that." I was flattered with these words from one of my African American first-semester Spanish students. As a Spanish teacher, I have plenty of opportunities to make connections to my students' lives and must do so to not only spark an interest in language learning, but to foster a stronger sense of self.

When the debate around Ebonics, or African American Vernacular English (AAVE), was at its peak, it seemed to be a moot point. Those that were clamoring for all students to speak Standard English didn't even speak it themselves. After all, in England they consider U.S. "Standard" English, American. The English most definitely don't give it the distinction of English. They claim Americans have changed spellings, adopted words from other languages, and clearly speak with an incorrect accent and intonation. Hmmm, sound familiar? Clearly what makes a language a "standard" is heavily influenced by what segment of society is in power.

As a Spanish teacher I see a similar debate with the many varieties of Spanish that have enriched the world. Perhaps the most "prestigious" form is that which is deemed "correct" by the Real Academia Española (the governing body in Spain that makes decisions of language use), yet multiple varieties of Spanish have evolved as a result of migration and interaction with other languages, just as English has evolved. Are we not to consider those "correct" as well? We speak what we speak as a result of who we are in an historical context. Therefore, how can any of us be "wrong"? That said, this does not mean that we shouldn't recognize that there is often a language variety that our society might consider a "standard" and that our students need to be proficient in to succeed. However, this should not happen at the expense of the language varieties that our respective communities value and that represent who we are culturally.

The opportunity for language teachers to value and respect the multiple language varieties of any language that are spoken, and more importantly, that our students speak, should be a focal point. I teach Spanish in an urban environment where many of my students have had to navigate two worlds, that of dominant society and their home cultures. Many speak AAVE comfortably and can switch to "Standard" English (or should I say "Standard American"?) when the context calls for it. Unfortunately, school have historically discredited their language and in effect, their cultures and their humanity. Think of the effect that it would have on you if you received subtle, and often not-so-subtle, messages that your language variety was bad. These messages have not only prevented teachers from having a broader understanding of issues surrounding linguistic diversity, but they have also had a negative impact on students' self-worth.

In my classroom, I tap into the rich linguistic diversity that exists in the Spanish-speaking world to make connections to the same phenomenon in the English-speaking world. It is not a unit, nor a particular lesson in which this happens, it is a part of the fabric of the class. It is impossible to consider why there is such tremendous linguistic diversity without understanding it in its historical contexts. It becomes quite easy to turn a lesson on why U.S. Spanish varies from other forms into an empowering lesson on why AAVE is not incorrect, sloppy, or bad, but rather a variety of English that has also evolved. Regardless of what we teach, it is important to consider knowledge in its historical contexts, and make the connections to our students' lives.

When comparing the many ways to express something in Spanish, depending on the context, we do the same in English. Although I do not speak AAVE, nor attempt to, the respect and validity it gets in my classroom has created an opportunity for students to feel respected and valued, and to have a stronger sense of who they are in a historical context.

TEACHER ACTION PROJECT: RESEARCHING LANGUAGE DIVERSITY IN SCHOOLS

Research the languages and dialects spoken in a school or in your community. Arrange to conduct your survey to coincide with Foreign Language Month, which is celebrated nationwide in March. The survey would yield valuable information about languages and dialects in the district or community as well as help to establish a database of students and community members who might be willing to serve as translators for English Language Learners and newcomers.

Here is a sample survey:

SAMPLE SURVEY

Dear Students, Parents, and Community Members,

In honor of Foreign Language Month and in the spirit of the United States Census, we would like your participation in this survey. Please circle the answer that best applies.

Do you speak a language or dialect other than Standard American English at home?   yes/no

What is this language? _____

How well do you speak the language?
very well   well   not well

Would you be willing to serve as a translator for new students who speak your language? yes/no

Name _____ grade _____

With the information gathered, create a report similar to the following and share it with your school and community. Establish a database of translators and "language buddies," for English Language Learners and newcomer students.

REPORT FOR JOHN ADAMS HS

About the Project

In honor of Foreign Language Month and in the spirit of the United States Census, the students, parents, and community members of John Adams Public School District were asked about the languages and dialects they speak at home. Surveys were distributed to students in their homeroom and World Language classes. Over one thousand surveys were collected and analyzed.

The Results of the Project

Approximately 53% of the students in the Middle and High Schools speak a language or dialect other than Standard American English at home (Figure 7.1).

Figure 7.1 Multilingual and monolingual student percentages.

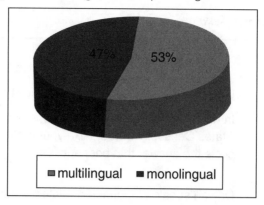

Figure 7.2 The district's most commonly spoken languages

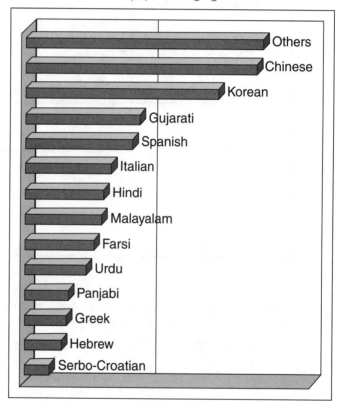

Chinese and Korean are the most commonly spoken languages (Figure 7.2).

The following languages are spoken in the John Adams community:

American Sign	Greek	Malayalam
Arabic	Gujarati	Panjabi
Bengali	Haitian Creole	Serbo-Croatian
Chinese (Cantonese)	Hebrew	Spanish
Chinese (Mandarin)	Hindi	Tagalog
Chinese (Taiwanese)	Italian	Tamil
English	Korean	Telugu
Farsi	Kutchi	Urdu

Figure 7.3 Student volunteer peer translators.

language	grade	students
Arabic	6	Salim Rabat, Ahmed Kofi
Bengali	9	Ziyad Dutta
	11	Tanzina Haque
Chinese (Cantonese)	6	Alexander Lu, Kelvin Wong, Wil Chu
	7	Teresa Lee, Chari Lai, Mike Hung
	11	Jessica Sung
Chinese (Mandarin)	7	Jennifer Choi, Harrison Chow, Adam Hu
	8	Andy Cheung

The preceeding students volunteered to serve as peer translators for new students (Figure 7.3).

References and Suggested Readings

Anzaldua, G. (1999). *Borderlands/La frontera: The new meztiza*. San Francisco: CA: Aunt Lute.

Castañeda, A. (1996). Language and other lethal weapons: Cultural politics and the rites of children as translators of culture. In A. Gordon & C. Newfield (Eds.), *Mapping multiculturalism* (pp. 201–204). Minneapolis: University of Minnesota Press.

Corson, D. (2001). *Language diversity and education*. Mahwah, NJ: Lawrence Erlbaum Associates.

Crawford, J. (2000). *At war with diversity: U.S. language policy in an age of anxiety*. Buffalo, NY: Multilingual Matters.

Cummins, J. (2001). *Language, power and pedagogy: Bilingual children in the crossfire*. Buffalo, NY: Multilingual Matters.

Delpit, L. (Ed.). (2003). *The skin that we speak: Thoughts on language and culture in the classroom*. New York: New Press.

Diaz Soto, L. (2002). *Making a difference in the lives of bilingual/bicultural children*. New York: Peter Lang.

Dueñas González, R. (Ed.). (2001). *Language ideologies: Critical perspectives on the official English movement*. Mahwah, NJ: Lawrence Erlbaum Associates.

Garcia, O., Skutnabb-Kangas, T., & Torres-Guzman, M. E. (Eds.). *Imagining multilingual schools: Language in education and glocalization*. Buffalo, NY: Multilingual Matters.

Goldstein, T. (2003). *Teaching and learning in a multilingual school: Choices, risks, and dilemmas*. Mahwah, NJ: Lawrence Erlbaum Associates.

Igoa, C. (1995). *The inner world of the immigrant child*. Mahwah, NJ: Lawrence Erlbaum Associates.

Kanno, Y. (2003). *Negotiating bilingual and bicultural identities: Japanese returnees betwixt two worlds*. Mahwah, NJ: Lawrence Erlbaum Associates.

McKay, S. L., & Wong, S. C. (Eds.). (2000). *New immigrants in the United States: Readings for second language educators*. New York: Cambridge University Press.

Nieto, S. (2002). *Language, culture, and teaching: Critical perspectives for a new century*. Mahwah, NJ: Lawrence Erlbaum Associates.

Olson, L., Bhattacharya, J., Chow, M., Dowell, C. (Ed.), Jaramillo, A., Tobiassen, D. P., & Solorio, J. (2001). *And still we speak. . . Stories of communities sustaining and reclaiming language and culture*. Oakland, CA: California Tomorrow.

Pérez, B., (Ed.). (2004). *Sociocultural contexts of language and literacy*. Mahwah, NJ: Lawrence Erlbaum Associates.

Phillipson, R. (2000). *Rights to language: Equity, power and education.* Mahwah, NJ: Lawrence Erlbaum Associates.

Pugach, M. (1998). *On the border of opportunity: Education, community, and language at the U.S.-Mexico line.* Mahwah, NJ: Lawrence Erlbaum Associates.

Santa Ana, O. (2004). *Tongue-tied: The lives of multilingual children in public education.* New York: Rowman & Littlefield.

Skutnabb-Kangas, T. (2000). *Linguistic genocide in education or worldwide diversity and human rights?* Mahwah, NJ: Lawrence Erlbaum Associates.

LESSON 19

TALKING WITH YOUR BODY

Go to the Take Action! DVD to view a video of this lesson, "Talking with Your Body," in action.

GRADE LEVELS

Grades K–5

CONTENT AREAS ADDRESSED

Language Arts, Visual Arts, World Languages

TOPIC

Gestures are viewed as culture specific in this lesson. Students explore different gestures and discuss how they differ in a variety of cultural contexts.

RATIONALE FOR USING THIS LESSON

Unlike many facial expressions, very few gestures are universally understood and interpreted. What is perfectly acceptable in the United States may be rude, or even obscene, in other cultures. It is important for mainstream teachers to understand how the gestures they use unconsciously may be misunderstood. This activity allows participants to look a little closer at how body language might be interpreted by English Language Learners and their parents.

BACKGROUND INFORMATION: BODY LANGUAGE— NATURE OR NURTURE?

Anthropologist Ray Birdwhistell (1970) claims that language is 35% of all communication while the rest is non-verbal. Anyone who has taken part in a conversation has reacted to non-verbal cues without, perhaps, being aware of doing so. For example, when a North American mother asks the question "Why did you do that?" of her small child in a scolding tone, a typical wordless reply might be the shrug of the child's shoulders. The mother immediately understands this gesture as "I don't know," as would most North Americans. In fact, there is *more* communicated with the gesture than "meets the eye." for the child most likely *does* know why she did what she did, but is being evasive. All of this information, text and subtext, was communicated by a simple gesture. North Americans would "read" the shrug in this way, but would members of another culture?

Conversations with a native speaker of a language other than English often yield differences in body language and proxemics—the physical space in interpersonal relationships (Nine Curt, 1984). For example, a stereotype regarding Italian speakers involves an abundant use of hand gestures. For Mexican children, it is not polite to make eye contact with their elders (Strong, 1983). To a Tunisian, the symbol made by joining the index finger and thumb means "I will kill you" while the same gesture in Japan represents money (Ferrieux, 1989). Thus gestures differ in their meanings from culture to culture, and even identical gestures might have different meanings. Gestures that make reference to an object which is not present are called "deictics" (McNeill, 1987). These are pointing motions, and represent the spatial location of persons, places or things (Brittan, 1996). By observing the manner in which a person represents a non-present entity, certain aspects of that person's culture are revealed. For instance, in Mexico it is considered disrespectful to point in a church, while in Indonesia, it is impolite to point in general. Observations such as these have the potential to shed light on the underlying belief system or worldview of a given culture.

(From Langer de Ramirez, L. (2003). "Symbolic gestures: Non-verbal communication in the classroom." *Language Magazine, 2*(9), 13–15)

Body-language signals may be learned, innate, or mixed. Eye-wink, thumbs-up, and military-salute gestures, for instance, are clearly learned. Eye-blink, throat-clear, and facial-flushing cues, on the other hand, are clearly inborn or innate. Laugh, cry, shoulder-shrug, and most other body-language signals are "mixed," because they originate as innate actions, but cultural rules later shape their timing, energy, and use. Body-language researchers do not always agree on the nature-nurture issue, however. Like Darwin, human biologists suppose that many body-motion signs are inborn. Like Birdwhistell, many cultural anthropologists propose that most or even all gestures are learned, while others combine the biological and cultural approaches. Research by psychologist Paul Ekman and his colleagues has shown that the facial expressions of disgust, surprise, and other primary emotions are universal across cultures.

(From Givens, D. B., Nonverbal Communication. Copyright © 1998–2005 Center for Nonverbal Studies, http://members.aol.com/nonverbal2/nvcom.htm)

References

Birdwhistell, R. L. (1970). *Kinesics and context.* Philadelphia: University of Pennsylvania.

Brittan, D. (1996). Talking hands. *Technology Review, 99*(3), 10.

Ferrieux, E. (1989). Hidden messages. *World Press Review, 36,* 39.

McNeill, D. (1987). *Psycholinguistics.* Cambridge, MA: Harper & Row.

Nine Curt, C. J. (1984). *Non-verbal communication.* Cambridge, MA: Evaluation, Dissemination and Assessment Center.

Strong, M. (1983). Social styles and the second language acquisition of Spanish-speaking kindergartners. *TESOL Quarterly, 17*(2), 241–258.

GOALS/AIMS

- Students will understand that the meaning of gestures differ depending on the culture that is interpreting them.

- Students will gain appreciation, respect, and acceptance of cultures different than their own.

- Students will increase their knowledge of traditions in a variety of cultures.

CONNECTIONS TO STANDARDS

- *Language Arts Reading Standard 7*: Uses reading skills and strategies to understand and interpret a variety of informational texts.

- *Visual Arts Standard 1*: Understands and applies media, techniques, and processes related to the visual arts.

- *Visual Arts Standard 4*: Understands the visual arts in relation to history and cultures.

- *World Language Standard 5*: Understands that different languages use different patterns to communicate and applies this knowledge to the target and native languages.

(Copyright 2007. Reprinted with permission from *Content Knowledge: A Compendium of Standards and Benchmarks for K-12 Education,* 4th ed. http://www.mcrel.org/standards-benchmarks/ All rights reserved.)

MATERIALS

- Copy of the books *Communication*, by Aliki (NY: Greenwillow, 1999), and *Simple Signs*, by Cindy Wheeler (NY: Penguin, 1997)
- Lesson 19 Resource Page 1: Gesture Checklist
- Lesson 19 Resource Page 2: Emotions Handout
- Digital or disposable camera
- Card stock or oak tag for posters
- A s to the Internet or printouts of a webpage with sign language images (i.e., http://www.planetavisual.net)

ACTIVITY

1. Read page 5 from the book *Communication*, by Aliki, to students. Ask students to identify the four gestures that are depicted in the middle of the page (after the text, "If we can't speak someone's language, we use body language"). The four gestures convey the following meanings:

    a. "I'm cold" or "It's cold in here."
    b. "Shhhh!" or "Be quiet!"
    c. "I'm hot" or "I'm hungry" (depending on whether students focus on the hand on the boy's stomach or on his head)
    d. "Would you like some food?"

2. Choose several pages from the book *Simple Signs*, by Cindy Wheeler, to share with students. Have students do the signs shown on the pages. Share signs in different languages with students to compare the differences and similarities. (Note: An excellent online dictionary for Spanish Sign Language can be found online at http://www.planetavisual.net—click on "diccionario.")

3. Ask students to think about gestures and body language. Explain to them that some gestures are universal—they are understood by almost everyone—but that many are used differently in different cultures.

4. Demonstrate the gestures depicted in Lesson 19 Resource Page 1 and ask students to put a checkmark in the smiley face column if the gesture is acceptable in the United States, or in the frowny face column if the gesture is considered rude. Older students should also think about and/or write down what the gesture might mean.

5. Share the results of the checklist with students. (Note: The information is written in language for teachers. Read the information for yourself and explain it to your students in your own words.) As you explain to students the cultural differences, show students where each country or region is on a map or a globe.

    a. In the United States, we tend to hold our hand with palm facing downward to express ideas such as "He's this big!" when referring to a child. In some parts of Latin America, this gesture is only used for animals and is considered rude for use with human beings. In Ecuador and Peru, the palm of the hand faces outward when measuring the height of a person. In Mexico, an outstretched finger is used.

    b. The head being shaken left to right in the United States can be considered a "no" or possibly a "maybe" response. In India and other parts of the subcontinent, when someone shakes their head in this way—or in a number 8 pattern—it is a gesture for "yes." While it is not considered rude in either culture, it can lead to a great deal of miscommunication when misinterpreted.

    c. Pointing at people is considered rude in many cultures around the world. There are other ways to point at people, for example, holding out your hand as if holding a plate or a head nod, as in South America.

    d. Pulling one's ears in the United States might not mean much, but in India, it is a sign of apology or humility. It is a gesture also used in the Hindu religion. In a Hindu temple, after knocking the temples lightly, devotees will often pull gently on the ear lobes with arms crossed, while bobbing up and down by bending the knees and bowing forward slightly. This gesture is an expression of humility, recognition that all souls are children in the eyes of God.

  e. In the United States, we tend to keep a bit of distance between us as we speak. In the Middle East, being too far away from your conversation partner can be perceived as a sign of mistrust.

6. Arrange students in small groups and ask them to label the Emotions Handout (Lesson 19 Resource Page 2) with the emotions that they think are being shown. Have students share their posters with the class. Are all the responses the same? Have students give ideas about why they think the answers were all the same or were different.

7. In the same small groups, have students invent a new gesture that means "hello." Encourage them to be creative and to try not to use a gesture that they are already familiar with.

8. Have each group share their new gesture with the class and explain why they chose the one that they did.

ACTION PROJECT

Have students take photos of gestures that represent the different cultures in the school—especially of ones that may have caused conflict or been misinterpreted in the past. Have them visit classes and interview students and teachers to "collect" gestures. Once they have a good selection, have them create some large posters for display around the school and also some $8\frac{1}{2} \times 11$ inch photocopiable posters for distribution to all the classrooms.

REFLECTION

Which gestures do you see students do every day that might be considered offensive? Are there any gestures that you use that you were surprised to find are considered rude in other cultures? What gestures that are acceptable in other cultures do you consider rude? Why do you think there is such a difference? What might these differences reveal?

Lesson 19 adapted from Judie Haynes' *Talking With Your Body*. Used with permission.

LESSON 19 RESOURCE PAGE 1: GESTURE CHECKLIST

Gesture	Not rude 🙂	Rude! 🙁
a.		
b. Yes No		
c.		
d.		
e.		

(Himalayan gesture of Humility adapted from the Himalayan Academy,
http://www.himalayanacademy.com/resources/books/lg/lg_ch-12.html. Used with permission)

LESSON 19 RESOURCE PAGE 2: EMOTIONS HANDOUT

How do you feel?

*Work with a partner to write the word for the emotion
that best describes each face.*

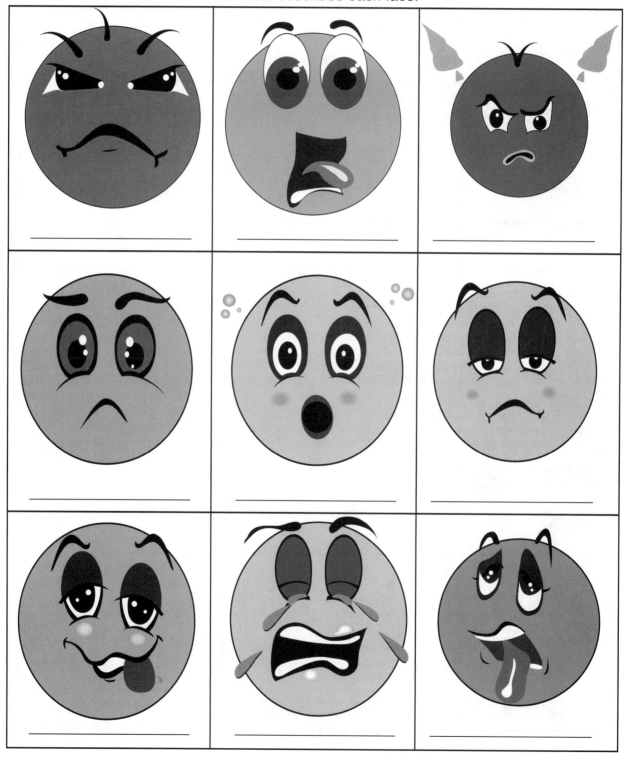

LESSON 20
ACCENT ON SPEECH

GRADE LEVELS

Grades 6–8

CONTENT AREAS ADDRESSED

Language Arts, Life Skills, Technology, World Language

TOPIC

Accents, word choice, and other markers of speech can lead to stereotyping and can also break down communication. Students learn about language by examining the sociolinguistic factors that affect communication.

RATIONALE FOR USING THIS LESSON

We begin the study of language before we ever learn to speak. Our perceptions of the world are influenced by the language used around us, yet in school the exploration of oral language is largely related to literacy skills such as phonics and decoding. Rarely do we consider with students the cultural implications of speech: accents, dialects, and the many different styles of speaking we utilize based on the situations we are in. For example, there is usually a difference between how students (particularly middle and high school students) address adults as opposed to their peers. Different fields require particular language, such as computer programming and medical fields. Even within the context of a single setting, we tend to make assumptions about people based on their choice of words and the way those words sound when spoken. Often it is the case that dialects and strong accents elicit the strongest biases. Do students find this to be the case? Why? This lesson can open the door to conversation about stereotypes linked to language as well as the purpose of learning to read and write what is considered standard academic English along with other forms.

BACKGROUND INFORMATION: FOCUS ON ACCENT: A SOCIOLINGUISTIC PERSPECTIVE OF DIVERSITY IN THE CLASSROOM

Past studies have shown that language differences, in accent and grammar, found in both native and foreign language speakers, elicit reactions in listeners that transfer over to judgments about the speakers' personalities. Throughout the world, stereotypic attitudes are commonly held towards groups of people in terms of such traits as race, gender, religion, and nationality. In the same vein, biases exist toward speakers of other languages or language varieties. It seems that people are very ready to judge others based on their speech.

Sociolinguistics is a field of study that looks at the connection between language and society. Dell Hymes, one of the pioneers of the field, believes that the structure of society may influence our use of, and attitudes toward, particular kinds of language, especially accents. Language may then be used to discriminate against and to control certain segments of society. Groups associated with a linguistic trait that is stigmatized (pronouncing aks for ask) are also stigmatized (Hymes, 1974; Newman, 2002). Sociolinguists would argue that there is nothing intrinsic to a linguistic feature that, on its own, makes it abhorrent. Instead, biases against a group are validated by devaluing certain linguistic markers associated with that group.

Some perceptions of speech quality do seem to be common in society. For example, English spoken with a foreign accent is labeled "broken" English (Reich, 2000). Even the speech of native speakers is vulnerable to judgment. Speech that has a good deal of nasal resonance is labeled unpleasant and unclear (Blood & Hyman, 1977). Speech with glottal sounds is labeled as harsh speech. Speech spoken quickly may be labeled pushy and aggressive (Tannen, 1990). Yes, a language may have certain nasalized sounds, glottal sounds, a particular rate and melody. These judgments about speech are more than descriptive, however, and they are often transferred to judgments about the speaker. Hence, the speakers are unpleasant, harsh, aggressive. Further, the process of judging and categorizing people by speech can be quite unconscious or even seem natural, something people would not question.

(From Behrens, S. J., & Neeman, A. R., Focus on accent: A sociolinguistic perspective of diversity in the classroom. *Research & Teaching in Developmental Education*, Spring 2004, http://www.findarticles.com/p/articles/mi_qa4116/is_200404/ai_n9465370)

References

Blood, G. W., & Hyman, M. (1977). Children's perception of nasal resonance. *Journal of Speech and Hearing Disorders, 42*, 446–448.

Hymes, D. (1974). *Foundations in sociolinguistics: An ethnographic approach.* Philadelphia: University of Pennsylvania Press.

Newman, B. (2002). Accent. *American Scholar, 71*(2), 59–69.

Reich, D. (2000). "Mother tongue" and standard English: Amy Tan's literary fusion and ours. In P. C. Hoy II & R. D. DiYanni (Eds.), *Encounters: Essays for explanation and inquiry,* 2nd ed. (pp. 74–76). Boston: McGraw Hill.

Tannen, D. (1990). *You just don't understand: Women and men in conversation.* New York: William Morrow.

GOALS/AIMS

- Students will be able to listen to recorded voices and make decisions based on what they hear.

- Students will understand the nature of speech and how it impacts the way we interact with people.

- Students will understand the cultural basis for accents and spoken language.

CONNECTIONS TO STANDARDS

- *Language Arts Listening Standard 8:* Uses listening and speaking strategies for different purposes.

- *Life Skills: Thinking and Reasoning Standard 2:* Understands and applies basic principles of logic and reasoning.

- *Life Skills: Thinking and Reasoning Standard 3:* Effectively uses mental processes that are based on identifying similarities and differences.

- *Technology Standard 3:* Understands the relationships among science, technology, society, and the individual.
- *World Language Standard 5:* Understands that different languages use different patterns to communicate and applies this knowledge to the target and native languages.

(Copyright 2007. Reprinted with permission from *Content Knowledge: A Compendium of Standards and Benchmarks for K-12 Education,* 4th ed. http://www.mcrel.org/standards-benchmarks/ All rights reserved.)

MATERIALS

- Lesson 20 Resource Page: Rating Scales
- Brief clips (not more than 1–2 minutes) of prerecorded speech from two or more different sources. The topic being discussed should be the same for all sources. These snippets of language should come from people with different accents, languages, or cultural backgrounds. You might record friends, colleagues, or even students from other classes. The voices might be asked to describe a funny, frustrating, or embarrassing incident. More important than the content is that the voices be distinct from one another and that you keep information about the person speaking for later identification. You can also use clips from movies, television commercials, the radio, books on tape, etc., but that will change the nature of the discussion slightly as scripts and literature are written to elicit particular responses, whereas everyday speech can elicit responses that the speaker may not be aware of or intend.

ACTIVITY

1. Have the class listen to the speakers without giving any information about them or your connection with them, if any. Give students time to reflect slightly to themselves after each clip. This reflection may be conducted in a number of different ways. Students can be asked to use a rating scale such as the one on Lesson 20 Resource Page. You might make up a different rating scale and/or tailor the list of adjectives and qualifiers to the specific voices you are using. Students could also be asked to generate their own list of phrases, draw a picture, or write a description of the person speaking. They might be asked to guess their occupations, rather than choosing from a list.

2. The class should then come together as a whole to discuss the assumptions made as well as why certain conclusions were drawn.

3. Finally, share the actual information about the speakers with the students. Ask students: How close were your guesses?

4. When activities such as this one are conducted with students, it is important to "debrief," or discuss the nature of the activity with them afterwards. In this case, students are being set up to stereotype and judge the voices on the recordings. This is a kind of manipulation that does not necessarily reflect how bias works in our day-to-day lives. Teachers should understand that this kind of activity is not meant to be isolated in the classroom, but carried out and considered in the context of interactions that take place outside of teacher instruction. Follow up by asking students about their participation—what they believe to be the purpose of the activity and what they will take away from the experience.

ACTION PROJECT

Have students collect their own samples of speech. Encourage students to record different accents and variations of speech and to document and take notes on the speakers. They might choose to look at specific types of language variants such as slang, the language development of younger siblings, or escalated speech (i.e., how language changes based on emotional content of the utterances). Have them conduct the same experiment (i.e., rating the speech clips) with their friends and family. Encourage them to write a school newspaper report or essay with their findings.

How did students react to the recorded voices? Did anything surprise you about their reactions? How did you feel to be "setting up" your students to make judgments about the voices? Do you think they would make these judgments even if not set up in this activity? Why or why not? Do you feel that it is ethical/worthwhile/important to manufacture an activity to prove a point to students? If so, when, or in what circumstances? If not, why not?

LESSON 20 RESOURCE PAGE: RATING SCALES

Voice # _____

What do you think of this person? (Put a check mark on a line on the scale to indicate your opinion.)

1. intelligent _____ _____ _____ _____ _____ not intelligent
2. active _____ _____ _____ _____ _____ not active
3. unfair _____ _____ _____ _____ _____ fair
4. truthful _____ _____ _____ _____ _____ untruthful etc . . .
5. good-looking _____ _____ _____ _____ _____ ugly
6. not comical _____ _____ _____ _____ _____ comical
7. not courageous _____ _____ _____ _____ _____ courageous
8. unsure _____ _____ _____ _____ _____ confident
9. likeable _____ _____ _____ _____ _____ hateful
10. reliable _____ _____ _____ _____ _____ unreliable
11. unsociable _____ _____ _____ _____ _____ sociable
12. short _____ _____ _____ _____ _____ tall
13. ambitious _____ _____ _____ _____ _____ not ambitious
14. friendly _____ _____ _____ _____ _____ unfriendly
15. religious _____ _____ _____ _____ _____ not religious
16. strong _____ _____ _____ _____ _____ weak
17. impolite _____ _____ _____ _____ _____ polite
18. happy _____ _____ _____ _____ _____ sad
19. selfish _____ _____ _____ _____ _____ not selfish
20. determined _____ _____ _____ _____ _____ not determined
21. How much do you feel you resemble this person?
    Very much _____ _____ _____ _____ _____ not at all
22. How much would you like to be like this person?
    Very much _____ _____ _____ _____ _____ not at all
23. In your opinion, what would likely be the occupation of this person? Choose one of the following:

    _____ radio announcer
    _____ lawyer
    _____ maid or janitor
    _____ bus driver
    _____ bank clerk
    _____ university or high school teacher

(From Lambert, W. E., Giles H., & Picard, O. (1975). Language attitudes in a French-American community. *International Journal of the Sociology of Language, 4,* 127–152.)

LESSON 21
THE GENGLISH-ONLY MOVEMENT

GRADE LEVELS

Grades 9–12

CONTENT AREAS ADDRESSED

Language Arts, Life Skills, Mathematics, Technology, World Language

TOPIC

There is no official language of the United States, but there are some groups who are fighting for "English Only." They advocate that all government and other business in this country be conducted solely in English, both oral and written). This lesson will walk students through a simulation in which they find themselves in the linguistic minority. The premise for the simulation involves an invasion of aliens who declare that the official language of the United States will be "Genglish." Through the activities in the lesson, students will feel firsthand the effects of legislated language use.

RATIONALE FOR USING THIS LESSON

According to the 1990 United States Census, 31.8 million U.S. residents, or 14 percent of the population 5 years old and over, reported they spoke a language other than English at home. These figures compare with 23.1 million persons or 11 percent in 1980 (http://www.census.gov). People who do not speak English in the United States face discrimination, financial challenges, and inequities on many levels. Despite many federal and state supports in place, students who are flagged as "English Language Learners" and given ESL (English as a Second Language) classes also face sometimes insurmountable challenges when they are expected to perform in an academic setting in a language that they have not yet mastered. This lesson will sensitize English-speaking students to the struggles that English Language Learners face—both in school and in society in general.

BACKGROUND INFORMATION: THE OFFICIAL ENGLISH MOVEMENT

At the time of Independence, America was populated by speakers of many languages, including English, German, French, Spanish, and hundreds of American Indian languages. When the founding fathers decided not to declare an official language, their reasons included "a belief in tolerance for linguistic diversity within the population, the economic and social value of foreign language knowledge and citizenry, and a desire not to restrict the linguistic and cultural freedom of those living in the new country" (Judd, 1987, p. 15). The issue of an official language has surfaced periodically throughout U.S. history but was not raised in Congress until 1981, when Senator S. I. Hayakawa of California introduced a constitutional amendment to make English the official language. On the surface, the idea appeared to be a symbolic gesture—to give English, the *de facto* language of the country, official status. However, the proposed amendment also called for prohibition of state laws, ordinances, orders, programs, and policies that require the use of other languages. Neither the federal government nor any state government could require any program, policy, or document that would use a language other than English.

The Official English movement seeks to make English the official language of the United States through passage of a constitutional amendment. Supporters argue that "in a pluralistic nation such as ours, government should foster the similarities that unite us, rather than the differences that separate us" (Wright, 1992, p. 129) and "unless we become serious about protecting our heritage as a unilingual society—bound by a common language—we may lose a precious resource that has helped us forge a national character and identity from so many diverse elements" (Chavez, 1987, p. 11). Providing education or services in other languages, it is feared, will give rise to ethnic separatism and the breakdown of national unity; the way to prevent this rift is to make English the official language.

The movement is spearheaded by two groups, English First and U.S. English. Goals of the movement are to encourage ratification of a constitutional amendment making English the official language of the United States; to repeal bilingual voting requirements; to reduce funding for bilingual education; to enforce English language and civics requirements for naturalization; and to expand opportunities for learning English (U.S. English, 1992).

Although the Senate convened hearings on Official English in 1984 and the House did so in 1988, the English Language Amendment has never come to a congressional vote. In 1991, Official English advocates took a different approach and launched a statutory form of Official English. Such legislation would apply to the Federal government alone and would require only a simple majority vote in Congress, in addition to the President's signature. This Language of Government bill has appeared in several versions, and one of these bills, H.R. 123, passed the House of Representatives in 1996. However, the companion measure never came to a vote in the Senate, and the bill died in the 104th Congress (Crawford, 1997b). A similar bill, also designated H.R. 123, is pending in the 105th Congress. If enacted, English would be designated the official language of the United States government, and the use of other languages in all federal government programs, publications, proceedings, and services would be outlawed—with a few exceptions for national security, language teaching, and the use of Native American languages (Crawford, 1997a).

(From Lewelling, V. W., Official English and English Plus: An update, May 1997, EDO-FL-97-07, ERIC Clearinghouse on Languages and Linguistics. http://www.cal.org/resources/digest/lewell01.html)

References

Chavez, L. (1987). *English: Our common bond.* Speech presented to the Los Angeles World Affairs Council, December 4.

Crawford, J. (1997a). English-only bill reintroduced in 105th Congress. English only update VIII. Available from http://ourworld.compuserve.com/homepages/JWCRAWFORD

Crawford, J. (1997b). Issues in U.S. language policy: Language legislation in the U.S.A. Available from http://ourworld.compuserve.com/homepages/JWCRAWFORD

Judd, E. L. (1987). The English Language Amendment: A case study on language rights. *TESOL Quarterly, 21*(1), n.p.

U.S. English. (1992). In defense of our common language. In J. Crawford (Ed.), *Language loyalties: A source book on the official English controversy* (pp. 143–147). Chicago: University of Chicago Press.

Wright, G. (1992). U.S. English. In J. Crawford (Ed.), *Language loyalties: A source book on the official English controversy* (pp. 127–128). Chicago: University of Chicago Press.

GOALS/AIMS

- Students will understand the inaccuracies of language stereotypes in society and their implications.
- Students will understand the effects of language discrimination and the role it plays in American culture and schools.
- Students will feel the effects of being a member of a linguistic minority.

CONNECTIONS TO STANDARDS

- *Language Arts Standard 4:* Adjusts use of spoken, written, and visual language (e.g., conventions, style, vocabulary) to communicate effectively with a variety of audiences and for different purposes.
- *Language Arts Standard 9:* Develops an understanding of and respect for diversity in language use, patterns, and dialects across cultures, ethnic groups, geographic regions, and social roles.
- *Life Skills—Working with others: Standard 1:* Contributes to the overall effort of a group.
- *Life Skills—Working with others: Standard 4:* Displays effective interpersonal communication skills.
- *Life Skills—Working with others: Standard 5:* Demonstrates leadership skills.
- *Mathematics Standard 6:* Understands and applies basic and advanced concepts of statistics and data analysis.
- *Mathematics Standard 8:* Understands and applies basic and advanced properties of functions and algebra. (Understands how graphs can represent patterns.)
- *Technology Standard 2:* Knows the characteristics and uses of computer software programs.
- *World Language Standard 5:* Understands that different languages use different patterns to communicate and applies this knowledge to the target and native languages.

(Copyright 2007. Reprinted with permission from *Content Knowledge: A Compendium of Standards and Benchmarks for K-12 Education*, 4th ed. http://www.mcrel.org/standards-benchmarks/ All rights reserved.)

MATERIALS

- Lesson 21 Resource Page: Newspaper Article
- Access to computers for word processing and Internet
- Access to video equipment for action project video

ACTIVITY

1. Set the stage for the simulation by telling students that you have to share some breaking news with them: the United States has been invaded by aliens and is now in their complete control. Our president has been replaced with an alien president, who has made several proclamations from the White House oval office. Have them read the mock newspaper article (Lesson 21 Resource Page).

2. In small groups, have students react to the article by brainstorming how they feel. Have each group share their reactions with the class. Create a class brainstorm on the board with the words and phrases generated.

3. Divide the students into groups according to different roles in society. Here are some possibilities:
   - Academics (i.e., students, teachers, college professors, etc.)
   - Government officials (i.e., mayors, governors, etc.)

- Blue-collar workers (i.e., plumbers, electricians, etc.)
- Homemakers (i.e., stay-at-home moms and dads, etc.)
- Artists (i.e., authors, actors, visual artists, etc.)

4. Have each student take on the role of a specific person. Ask the students to write a brief autobiography with the "backstory" of their character. The story should include details such as their name, profession, age, family, etc.

5. Ask students to take on the identity of their person and react orally in the group about the Genglish-only proclamation. Have each student explain their feelings about the new law and discuss in what ways the law will change their lives.

6. Have each group write a position statement about the proclamation. The statement might include reactions to the announcement, ways in which people will be affected, proposed changes to the law, and so forth. Have each group share their position paper with the class.

7. As a followup assignment (for homework or the following day) have students write a journal entry describing how their lives would change if they were required to speak a language other than English in school, at the mall, online when text messaging their friends, and so on. What would they do to learn the language? How do they think they would function in school?

8. Share information with students about the English-only movement from the background information. Encourage them to do research online about the movement and countermovements. Have students debate the different sides to the argument for and against an official language in the United States. You may refer them to the following two websites, with opposing views on the topic: U.S. English, Inc.: http://www.us-english.org/inc/andNational Council of La Raza: http://www.nclr.org/

ACTION PROJECT

Have students conduct interviews of people of different backgrounds regarding English and its importance in the United States. Here are some sample questions they might use in their survey:

1. Do you think English should be made the official language of the United States? Why or why not?

2. Do you think efforts should be made to allow other languages official status? If yes, which language(s)? Why?

Participants in the survey show a range of home languages, ages and occupations as shown in figure 7.4.

Figure 7.4 Language survey results.

NAME	Rodrigo	Leroy	Fabiola	Rose
NATIVE LANGUAGE	Spanish	English	Italian	English
YEARS IN U.S.	10	61	36	23
EDUCATION	one year undergraduate	three years undergraduate	three years postgraduate study	high school graduate
AGE	31	61	50	23
OCCUPATION	manager of laundromat	school janitor	foreign language teacher	housewife/ mother

Rodrigo: Yes, because it is part of the identity and culture of the country. It would be less confusing to have one official language, especially concerning legal matters.

Leroy: Yes, because it has always been the language of the United States.

Fabiola: Yes, because English has naturally been the language in the history of this country.

Rose: Yes, because that's the language that we speak here. I feel that immigrants should be able to speak English. This is not to say that they should lose their own heritage or culture, but this is America.

3. Do you think efforts should be made to allow other languages official status? If yes, which language(s)? Why?

Rodrigo: No, because too many languages would separate different language groups. Instead, with one official language, it doesn't really matter what specific language a person speaks, we would all be able to communicate.

Leroy: Yes, I think that Spanish and French should be made official languages in the United States. because Spanish is a culture close to the United States and French is a beautiful language!

Fabiola: No, what for? My concept of an official language is a native language. This means one language. A nation such as this needs to identify with something in common, in this case the language.

Rose: No. It would be a lot more expensive to print everything in other languages. People should learn how to speak other languages or they shouldn't come here.

4. Do you think children should be taught in a language other than English? Explain.

Rodrigo: No. By teaching the child in English, it would put the necessary pressure on the child to learn in English. However, children should be encouraged to learn other languages.

Leroy: No. Children should be taught in English in the United States.

Fabiola: Yes, but this should be restricted by regional or situational needs. For example, it may be necessary to teach a new group of immigrants in their native language. Bilingual learning may be helpful, but only as a temporary measure. Then ESL classes should be the next step.

Rose: No. I think they should learn English. They are in America. If they want to learn more, they should go to special classes to help them, but in English.

5. Do you think Americans speak English well? (If no, who does?)

Rodrigo: Yes. My first encounter with English was in the United States. I could not compare American English with other English-speaking cultures.

Leroy: Yes. Some Americans speak English well (some don't).

Fabiola: No. I am referring to linguistic problems in the educational system of this country. This is not to say that English from England is any better or worse than American English. It, of course, has its own legitimacy as a language.

Rose: Yes, but not in New York. I think they speak better in England. We use too many slang words in the United States.

6. Do you think the English language in the United States needs to be protected? (If yes, from whom?)

Rodrigo: No.

Leroy: No.

Fabiola: No. It self-protects when it is labeled as the official language.

Rose: It's not fair to foreign speaking people, but we let them into our country; they should have to learn English, not only so that they can understand us, but so that we can understand them. Yes, English needs to be protected in that sense.

REFLECTION

How do you feel about languages and dialects other than Standard American English (SAE) in the classroom? What experiences have you had with speakers of dialects or languages other than SAE? How do you feel about a student using nonstandard English in a classroom oral presentation? In an essay? In creative writing? What role do you feel nonstandard dialects and languages other than English should play in your classroom? In your school? In your community?

LESSON 21 RESOURCE PAGE: NEWSPAPER ARTICLE

President Hedge Proclaims Genglish as the New Official Language of the United States of Genlandia

English speakers enroll in Genglish classes across the country

As of 12 noon today, President Hedge has established the highly evolved and superior language of Genglish as the official language of the United States of Genlandia. From now on, all official transactions, government work, schools, and businesses must be conducted in Genglish or be subject to stiff fines or even imprisonment. Citizens across the country are overjoyed with this news, reports say.

Immediately following President Hedge's glorious announcement, the Undersecretary for the Acquisition of Genglish appropriated billions of dollars for school programs and classes in the Genglish language. Students in all 50 states will be required to take mandated state exams in Genglish as of next year. They will be given support classes, specialized placement testing, and other accommodations for the first year, after which time they will be required to take all subject courses and exams in the Genglish language. Educators and students alike applaud the announcement, stating: Genglish will unite the diverse peoples of this wonderful country. Long live Genglish!

CHAPTER 8

GENDER AND GENDER ROLES

Sugar and spice and everything nice,
That's what little girls are made of.
Snips and snails and puppy dog tails,
That's what little boys are made of.

(Popular rhyme)

Some Background

Think for a moment about your favorite friends from high school or college. Who were most memorable? What faces stand out for you as being the most special, funny, bright? Are they girls or boys? Are your most memorable female friends respectful? Talkative? Creative? Are your most memorable male friends smart? Competitive? Leaders?

We all have ideas about what is acceptable for girls and for boys and it is normal for these ideas to play a role in the classroom setting. Society has a way of instilling in us from a very young age the rules for playing the gender game. If gender roles were not important to us as a society as a whole, why would the first question for newborns be, "Is it a girl or a boy?"

It is important that we as teachers look critically at several issues relating to gender in the classroom (Hernández Sheets, 2005):

- *Social context of gender* = culturally appropriate ways of behaving
- *Gender identity* = the personal sense of being male or female
- *Gender roles* = the public expressions of gender identity displayed through choices, actions, and sex roles

We—teachers and students alike—constantly make unconscious decisions about gender appropriateness of behaviors. We educators also make our own choices about our roles as male or female teachers. Being more conscious of the ways in which gender is being played out in our classrooms is an important first step to creating accepting and safe environments for all students.

Lesson Preparation for the Teacher

ONE TEACHER'S REFLECTION—GENDER AND SCHOOL

My grandparents were a big part of the first decade of my life. They were the ever-willing babysitters who watched us on the occasional Saturday night that my parents wanted to see a movie. Grandma let us make all sorts of inventions in her kitchen and we got to stay up late to watch TV, all out of sight of Grandpa. Grandpa was a cranky person, who loved us in his own way, but was far from affectionate or indulgent. He let Grandma take care of us, and rarely joined us. Since Grandpa went to bed early and snored, Grandma slept in a different room and we used to snuggle together, drinking pink lemonade and vanilla ice cream floats, eating Doritos and watching the Carol Burnett Show. *In Grandma's love and warmth and Grandpa's frequent coldness, I think I began to delineate the genders into female as caring, loving, protector and male as indifferent and sometimes gruff.*

I still remember the small home converted into a school that was to be the scene of my first "traditional" classroom: my preschool. I remember playing with everyone and creating things. I loved the cubbyholes for our coats and the stories that the teachers read to us, but I remember loving the teachers the most. I loved to look at them and to hear their voices. They were all women and I think saw them as extensions of my own mother (who was also a teacher). I felt comfortable with them and I sought their approval and affection. Looking back, I realize that this first exposure to "outside" schooling must have solidified some image of the teacher as nurturer/mother in my mind.

When it was time to enter kindergarten, I was excited and eager to find another mother figure in my teacher. Mrs. Lauder did not disappoint. She was a creative, caring, and encouraging teacher and I loved her from the first day of class. I often think back to this time of my life in order to analyze questions of favoritism, model students, and other such classroom identity issues. I was decidedly Mrs. Lauder's favorite. She gave glowing reports to my parents of my talents, my excellent behavior, and my creativity. She told my mother that I reminded her of her own daughter. I was even given the coveted lead role of Gretel in our class production of Hansel and Gretel. Whether Mrs. Lauder really saw me as a star, or simply liked the way I liked her, I suddenly became aware of being teacher's pet, and cognizant of the fact that I loved it.

I always wonder if my unconditional love of Mrs. Lauder at the outset caused her to look upon me favorably as a student. Mrs. Lauder, though a patient woman in general, had some problems with some of the boys in the class. I now try to explore this gender issue in relation to my own teaching. How do my own students become my favorites? As much as I try to be fair and equal with my praise, do they know who I secretly like best?

TEACHER ACTION PROJECT: OBSERVING HIDDEN GENDER PREFERENCES

Visit a teaching colleague to observe a class. Watch your colleague's interactions with male and female students in the class and note any patterns. Keep a running tally of the times your colleague calls on boys or girls. (It would be helpful to observe on several occasions so that the teacher is not overly aware of your presence as an observer and is being as natural as possible when teaching.)

Review your impressions with your colleague. Does this teacher call more frequently on boys or on girls? How would you describe their interactions with boys? With girls? When a student doesn't know an answer, is the teacher's "wait time" longer for girls or for boys? What kinds of assumptions might be behind any differences? Is this teacher male or female?

References and Suggested Readings

Belenky, M. F., Clinchy, B. M., Goldberger, N. R., & Tarule, J. M. (1986). *Women's ways of knowing: The development of self, voice and mind.* New York: Basic Books.

Bettis, P., & Adams, N. (Eds.). (2005). *Geographies of girlhood: Identities in-between.* Mahwah, NJ: Lawrence Erlbaum Associates.

Fausto-Sterling, A. (2000). *Sexing the body: Gender politics and the construction of sexuality.* New York: Basic Books.

Frye, M. (1992). *Race, class and gender in the United States.* New York: St. Martin's.

Glennon, W. (1999). *200 ways to raise a girl's self-esteem.* Boston: Conari.

Glennon, W. (2000). *200 ways to raise a boy's emotional intelligence.* Boston: Conari.

Gore, J. M. (1993). *The struggle for pedagogies: Critical and feminist discourses as regimes of truth.* New York: Routledge.

Harris Scholastic Research. (1993). *Hostile hallways: The AAUW survey on sexual harassment in America's schools.* Washington, DC: American Association of University Women Foundation.

Hernández Sheets, R. (2005). *Diversity pedagogy: Examining the roles of culture in the teaching-learning process.* Boston: Allyn & Bacon.

Johansson, T. (2007). *The transformation of sexuality: Gender and identity in contemporary youth culture.* Burlington, VT: Ashgate.

Kindlon, D., & Thompson, M. (2000). *Raising Cain: Protecting the emotional life of boys.* New York: Ballantine.

Kleinfeld, J., & Yerian, S. (1995). *Gender tales: Tensions in the schools.* Mahwah, NJ: Lawrence Erlbaum Associates.

Lorber, J. (1994). *Paradoxes of gender.* New Haven: Yale University Press.

Maher, F., & Ward, J. (2002). *Gender and teaching.* Mahwah, NJ: Lawrence Erlbaum Associates.

Morris Schaffer, S., & Perlman Gordon, L. (2000). *Why boys don't talk and why we care: A mother's guide to connection.* Chevy Chase, MD: Mid-Atlantic Equity Consortium.

Okin, S. M., with Cohen, J., Howard, M., & Nussbaum, M. C. (Eds.). (1999). *Is multiculturalism bad for women?* Princeton, NJ: Princeton University Press.

O'Reilly, P., Penn, E., & deMarrais, K. (2001). *Educating young adolescent girls.* Mahwah, NJ: Lawrence Erlbaum Associates.

Pipher, M. (1994). *Reviving Ophelia: Saving the selves of adolescent girls.* New York: Ballentine.

Romaine, S. (1999). *Communicating gender.* Mahwah, NJ: Lawrence Erlbaum Associates.

Sadker, M., & Sadker, D. (1994). *Failing at fairness: How our schools cheat girls.* New York: Touchstone.

Sanders, J., Koch, J., & Urso, J. (1997). *Gender equity right from the start.* Mahwah, NJ: Lawrence Erlbaum Associates.

Taylor, D., & Lorimer, M. (2002). Helping boys succeed. *Educational Leadership, 60*(4), 68–70.

Thorne, B. (1993). *Gender play: Girls and boys in school.* Piscataway, NJ: Rutgers University Press.

LESSON 22

BURSTING GENDERALIZATIONS

GRADE LEVELS

Grades 3–6

CONTENT AREAS ADDRESSED

Language Arts, Visual Arts

TOPIC

Stereotypes abound regarding the appropriate roles for boys and girls, men and women. This lesson will encourage students to think critically about "genderalizations"—gender-related stereotypes and biases—and how they are used in the school setting.

RATIONALE FOR USING THIS LESSON

By the time they reach school age, young children already have a keen sense of what it means to be a boy or a girl. Messages reach them from all angles—from television, picturebooks, teachers and family, friends, and others. Speaking openly about these messages and how children feel about them can help them to move beyond stereotypes and to define their gender identities for themselves.

BACKGROUND INFORMATION: WHY DO MYTHS PERSIST?

Myths based on gender and on race persist, despite the evidence to the contrary. So where did they come from and why do they continue? The following are just some of the reasons:

I. History

It is a common belief that because men are the principal producers in "modern" society that this has always been the case. In fact in earlier times, when women were the main food gatherers and producers, there were matriarchal societies where women had high status, were preeminent as cultivators, and were glorified as goddesses. As late as the 2nd century BC, the major deities in European culture were women.

There are a variety of theories as to why this changed. Some like Reed felt that with the evolution of private property women lost their place in productive, social and cultural life and their worth sank along with their former status. Others like DeBeauvoir felt that change occurred when it was established that men as well as women were involved in the reproductive process. . . .

Researchers also used women's reproductive capacity to conclude women's intellectual inferiority, and then turned around and concluded that using the intellect would destroy reproductive capacity. For example:

Female students were concluded to be pale, in delicate health and "prey to monstrous deviations from menstrual regularity" (Clarke, 1873, last printing 1963).

Women are "closer to children and savages than to an adult civilized man." (Le Bon, 1879, reported in Gould, 1981).

At times in history it has been said that women are better than men. At other times it has been said that men are better than women. Both are wrong.

II. Research's Emphasis on Differences

Social science research is based on a search for differences. Since we don't look for similarities, we don't find them and thus perpetuate an overemphasis on the differences between girls and boys.

Differences are at the basis of research design and theory. Differences can be proved while similarities cannot. The concept of "statistically significant differences" is widely accepted and used—there is no general concept of statistically significant similarities. Thus in a research study, if you find differences, you have something. Your research is more likely to be seen as meaningful, and it is more likely to be published than it would be if you didn't find differences.

Finding similarities isn't currently an option, regardless of what your data say.

When research focuses on differences and when differences are all that is reported, difference-based stereotypes are reinforced and continued.

III. The Allure of Oversimplification

Complexity is hard, simplicity is easy. To deal with complexity we often revert to simplicity—we tend to categorize and make judgments based on that categorization.

Stereotypes are easy to fall into. When we see a woman do something really stupid in a car, many of us say "woman driver"; but when we see Lyn St. James win Rookie of the Year at the Indianapolis 500, very few of us say, "Wow, is that woman driver stereotype wrong." Thus are stereotypes reinforced, but rarely countered.

Is It Real or Is It a Stereotype?

It's a stereotype if it ascribes characteristics to an individual based solely on group membership. For example, it is a stereotype to assume a tall thin young African American male is a basketball player or that an Asian student is good in math.

It's probably a stereotype if it describes how girls and boys are "supposed" to be. For example, the statement that "Susie will be better than Ed at babysitting because she is a girl" is a stereotype.

It's probably a stereotype if a book, toy or tool is described or pictured as "for boys" or "for girls." For example, a chemistry set that only pictures boys is stereotypic; a book about growing up that is listed as "for boys" is not necessarily stereotypic although it may have stereotypes in it.

(From Campbell, P. B., & Storo, J. N. (1994.) *Girls are . . . Boys are . . .: Myths, stereotypes & gender differences.* Report for the Office of Educational Research and Improvement, U.S. Department of Education. Retrieved June 14, 2007 from http://www.campbell-kibler.com/Stereo.pdf)

References

Clark, E. H. (1963). *Sex in education or fair chance for girls.* Boston: James R. Osgood. (Reprinted Arno Press, 1972.)

Gould, S. (1981). *The mismeasure of man.* New York: W. W. Norton.

GOALS/AIMS

- Students will be able to define the term *stereotype.*
- Students will gain a deeper understanding of how stereotypes begin.
- Students will experience the injustice of stereotypes.

CONNECTIONS TO STANDARDS

- *Language Arts Writing Standard 1:* Uses general skills and strategies of the writing process.
- *Language Arts Writing Standard 4:* Gathers and uses information for research purposes.
- *Visual Arts Standard 1:* Understands and applies media, techniques, and processes related to the visual arts.
- *Visual Arts Standard 4:* Understands the visual arts in relation to history and cultures.

(Copyright 2007. Reprinted with permission from *Content Knowledge: A Compendium of Standards and Benchmarks for K-12 Education,* 4th ed. http://www.mcrel.org/standards-benchmarks/ All rights reserved.)

MATERIALS

- Lesson 22 Resource Page: Word Association
- One large pin
- One bulletin board and tacks
- Many inflated balloons
- Many precut paper strips
- Poster paper
- Magazines for cutting out pictures/images
- Scissors
- Glue

ACTIVITY

1. Give students a copy of Lesson 22 Resource Page. Ask them to draw a circle around words that make them think of boys, a square around words that make them think of girls, and underline words that make them think of both—or neither—boys or girls. Have volunteers share their answers with the class.

2. Write the word *stereotype* on the board and ask students if they have heard it before or know what it means. Brainstorm all the words and responses with the students and write their thoughts on the board to create a class definition.

3. Write a "genderalization" (a generalization about one gender) on the board, such as, "All boys are good at sports." Ask students if they can prove that this stereotype is not always true.

4. Ask students to share their feelings and reactions to stereotypes. Discuss the idea that generalizations and stereotypes are too general to be true all the time and provide counterexamples. Encourage students to recognize why these sweeping statements are unfair.

5. Divide students into small groups and ask them to create lists of stereotypes pertaining to gender that they have heard.

6. Ask each group to share the stereotypes on their list and choose a few to discuss with the class. Write each stereotype chosen on a strip of paper and attach it to the bulletin board with an inflated balloon. Ask if anyone can disprove or "break" the stereotype. The student who is able to do so will be given the pin and asked to break that stereotype's balloon.

7. Repeat step 6 for each stereotype that students have brainstormed. Discuss with students the unfairness and pain associated with the use of stereotypes, referring to the "broken" examples.

8. Develop a class motto or rules that includes statements about acceptance and avoidance of stereotypes. Post the proclamation in the classroom for all to see.

ACTION PROJECT

Have the class develop an anti-genderalizations poster for the classroom. The poster should include images and text. Encourage students to brainstorm a list of positive statements that counter the stereotypes that were discussed in the class. Some possible statements:

- Girls are great at math and science!
- Boys can take care of each other!
- Girls are good at sports!

REFLECTION

How do stereotypes reveal themselves among students? Among parents? Among teachers? Are there any "good" stereotypes? If so, which ones?

LESSON 22

RESOURCE PAGE: WORD ASSOCIATION

Look at this list of words.

- Draw a circle around words that make you think of boys.
- Put a check next to the words that make you think of girls.
- Underline words that make you think of both—or neither—boys or girls.

Adjectives	Nouns	Verbs
strong	sports	read
funny	cooking	study
smart	doctor	talk
caring	teacher	run
friendly	plumber	smile
obedient	scientist	dance
serious	librarian	jump

Lesson 21 adapted from Melissa Pesce's *Bursting Genderalization*. Used with permission.

LESSON 23

ROSALIND FRANKLIN— THE OTHER DISCOVERER OF DNA

Go to the Take Action! DVD to view a video of this lesson, "Rosalind Franklin—The Other Discoverer of DNA," in action.

GRADE LEVELS

Grades 6–8

CONTENT AREAS ADDRESSED

Language Arts, Science, Technology

TOPIC

Rosalind Franklin is a popular figure for teaching the notion of gender inequity in the sciences. This stems from the fact that she was closely involved in a major scientific event: the discovery of DNA. She was subjected to discrimination as were many women and African Americans who, for many years, were not considered to be worthy of full membership in the scientific community. The men working with Franklin (Wilkins, Gosling, Watson, and Crick) truly seemed threatened by her status as a woman.

RATIONALE FOR USING THIS LESSON

This lesson brings to light the challenges and inequities faced by women in science. It also portrays the fierce and often drama-filled competition that occurs when multiple scientists or labs are all vying to seek a common answer to a question or process. Furthermore, it provides a detailed explanation of the fascinating story that yielded the seminal biological discovery of the twentieth century. Franklin is an excellent role model for girls who are interested in science, as well as an unfortunate example of the challenges that female scientists have faced.

BACKGROUND INFORMATION: WHO IS ROSALIND FRANKLIN?

Nearly half a century ago, scientists raced to discover the secret of life. At the forefront of this effort was a brilliant British researcher who brought her substantial gifts to the study of DNA. Her name was Rosalind Franklin.

Born into an upper middle-class Jewish family in 1920, Rosalind Franklin was educated at a private school in London where she studied physics and chemistry from an early age, at an advanced level, especially so for a woman at that time. An excellent and dedicated student, undeterred by the social standard usually set for women, she earned a Ph.D. in physical chemistry in 1945 from Cambridge University.

She then spent four years at the *Laboratoire Central des Services Chimiques de L'Etat*, in Paris. It was there that she learned the techniques of X-ray crystallography, the scientific method that would lead to the discovery of a lifetime.

Early in her career, it was Rosalind Franklin who painstakingly conceived of and captured "Photograph 51" of the "B" form of DNA in 1952 while at King's College in London. It is this photograph, acquired through 100 hours of X-ray exposure from a machine Dr. Franklin herself refined, that revealed the structure of DNA and the key to understanding how the blueprint of all life on earth is passed down from generation to generation. Never before had X-ray crystallography—a technique of determining a molecule's three-dimensional structure by analyzing the X-ray diffraction patterns of crystals made up of the molecule in question—been put to such deft or momentous use.

The discovery of the structure of DNA was the single most important advance of modern biology. Decoding the structure of DNA put us on a path to understanding the human genome. Quite simply, it changed the future of healthcare forever. James Watson and Francis Crick, working at Cambridge University, used Photograph 51 as the basis for their famous model of DNA.

Rosalind Franklin went on to perform exceptional research at Birkbeck College. She died in 1958 of ovarian cancer, at age 37, perhaps from radiation exposure from her work, or perhaps due to her own genetic makeup. One thing is certain—she died without ever knowing the true magnitude of her contribution to the science of life.

Watson and Crick went on to win the Nobel Prize in 1962 for their DNA model—a model that was made possible by the magnificent work of Rosalind Franklin.

(From the Rosalind Franklin University website. Retrieved June 14, 2007 from http://www.lifeindiscovery.com/whyrosalindfranklin/index.html)

GOALS/AIMS

- Students will be able to identify Rosalind Franklin and understand how she contributed to the discovery of the double helix.
- Students will be able to understand the reasons why Franklin is not as well known as Watson and Crick.
- Students will be able to recognize and explain Rosalind Franklin's contribution to the elucidation of DNA structure.
- Students will discuss how gender biases hampered her work and contributed to the lack of recognition of her work in her lifetime.

CONNECTIONS TO STANDARDS

- *Language Arts Writing Standard 1:* Uses general skills and strategies of the writing process.
- *Language Arts Writing Standard 4:* Gathers and uses information for research purposes.
- *Language Arts Listening and Speaking Standard 8:* Uses listening and speaking strategies for different purposes.
- *Language Arts Viewing Standard 9:* Uses viewing skills and strategies to understand and interpret visual media.
- *Science Standard 5:* Life Sciences: Understands the structure and function of cells and organisms.
- *Science Standard 11:* Nature of Science: Understands the nature of scientific knowledge.
- *Science Standard 12:* Nature of Science: Understands the nature of scientific inquiry.
- *Science Standard 13:* Nature of Science: Understands the nature of scientific enterprise.
- *Technology Standard 1:* Knows the characteristics and uses of computer hardware and operating systems.
- *Technology Standard 2:* Knows the characteristics and uses of computer software programs.

(Copyright 2007. Reprinted with permission from *Content Knowledge: A Compendium of Standards and Benchmarks for K-12 Education*, 4th ed. http://www.mcrel.org/standards-benchmarks/ All rights reserved.)

MATERIALS

- Model or photo of DNA
- Excerpts from Watson's book *The Double Helix* (New York: Athaneum, 1968)
- Photos of Rosalind Franklin
- Lesson 23 Resource Page: Famous Women in Science

ACTIVITY

1. Have students write or discuss their responses to the following questions: Have you ever had an experience where someone took credit for work that you did? How did you feel about it? Briefly discuss responses to the questions with students.

2. Show a model of DNA. Ask students if they recognize it. Review the structure of DNA. Discuss the significance of DNA with students.

3. Questions for discussion:
   - Who is responsible for discovering the structure of DNA?
   - How did Watson and Crick find the structure?

4. Describe Franklin's work and how Watson and Crick used her results to make their model. As you discuss her contributions to the discovery of DNA, be careful to refer to her as "Dr. Franklin" and to not use gender-specific pronouns. Ask the students: "Why do you think Dr. Franklin didn't get credit for helping to find the structure of DNA?" Discuss.

5. Reveal a picture of Franklin. At this point, discussion is likely to go in any of several directions. Use the following, as appropriate:
   - Did you assume that Dr. Franklin was a man? Why?
   - Do you think Dr. Franklin was denied credit because she was a woman? Why?
   - Do you think Dr. Franklin would have received the Nobel Prize if she had lived?

6. Read excerpts from *The Double Helix*. Be sure to include negative portrayals as well as Watson's epilogue. Discuss students' reactions.

7. Questions for discussion:
   - How does Watson portray of Franklin in his book?
   - Why do you think Watson chose to portray Franklin in this way?
   - What do you think might have happened if Franklin had not died so young?
   - Why do you think there were so many challenges for female scientists in the 1950s?

8. Culminating activities: Give students a choice of research project. Some possibilities:
   - Have students research and create brief presentations on famous women scientists of the early twentieth century—what they accomplished, as well as challenges they faced (see Lesson 23 Resource Page for scientists to research).
   - Have students investigate the Secret of Photo 51 website (http:www.pbs.org/wgbh/nova/photo51). There is an excellent explanation of how Franklin's photo was interpreted to yield the double helix model.
   - Have students read excerpts from three selected *Nature* articles from 1953 published by Watson and Crick; Franklin and Gosling; and Wilkins, Stokes, and Wilson (http://www.nature.com/nature/dna50/archive.html). Compare and contrast the tone of these articles—why does Watson and Crick's seem so confident and flamboyant compared to the Franklin and Gosling and Wilkins et al. articles?

ACTION PROJECT

Have students think about someone they know who is working in a profession that is traditionally meant for the opposite gender (i.e., a man who is doing traditionally "woman's work," or a woman who is successful in a male-dominated field). This person might be a family member, someone in school, or a community member. Ask students to develop a list of interview questions for this person regarding the obstacles (if any) they faced in working in their field. Some possible questions:

- What made you interested in your line of work?
- What did you do to prepare yourself for work in your field? (i.e., what kind of training/schooling was necessary?)
- Did you face any obstacles in joining your field?
- What challenges, if any, do you face now?
- Do you think that progress has been made in leveling the playing field for men/women in your profession in the past years? Do you think more progress can/should made? Please explain.
- What advice would you give to a girl or boy who would like to follow in your footsteps?

Have students take a photo of their interviewee and write a brief biography about them. Create a class or school display with the information.

REFLECTION

Does gender stereotyping exist in your school? Think about your school's system of course selection and/or tracking. Are there different expectations of female versus male students in their choice of advanced science and math classes? Describe the gender makeup of your most challenging programs in school (i.e., the gifted program, honors courses, etc.). Are there any patterns that might reveal gender stereotyping? If so, what are those stereotypes?

LESSON 23

RESOURCE PAGE: FAMOUS WOMEN IN SCIENCE

- Rosalind Elsie Franklin—Molecular biologist
- Dorothy Crowfoot Hodgkin—Chemist; a founder of protein crystallography
- Grace Murray Hopper—Computer scientist
- Maria Goeppert-Mayer—Physicist; Nobel laureate
- Helen Sawyer Hogg—Astronomer
- Rózsa Péter—Mathematician; founder of recursive function theory
- Roger Arliner Young—Zoologist
- May Edward Chinn—Physician
- Emmy Noether—Mathematician
- Lise Meitner—Physicist
- Lillian Moller Gilbreth—Engineer and an industrial psychologist; "the mother of modern management"
- Annie Jump Cannon—Astronomer; theorist of star spectra
- Rosa Smith Eigenmann—Ichthyologist
- Ada Byron, Countess of Lovelace—Analyst, metaphysician, and founder of scientific computing
- Mary Anning—Fossil hunter
- Sophie Germain—Mathematician

(For information on these women, visit http://www.sdsc.edu/ScienceWomen)

Lesson 22 adapted from Michael Orlep & Maya Ban's *Rosalinkd Franklin - The Other Discoverer of DNA*. Used with permission.

LESSON 24

GENDER IN THE MEDIA—IMPLICIT MESSAGES

Grades 9–12

CONTENT AREAS ADDRESSED

Language Arts, Technology, Visual Arts, World Language

TOPIC

Gender roles are portrayed and reinforced in the popular media. These roles often go unfiltered and become part of our unexamined psyche.

RATIONALE FOR USING THIS LESSON

This lesson strives to make students more aware of the portrayal of these roles and to encourage them to be more critical of these portrayals through journals and an online implicit reaction test.

BACKGROUND INFORMATION: MEASURING IMPLICIT ASSOCIATIONS

Psychologists understand that people may not say what's on their minds either because they are *unwilling* or because they are *unable* to do so. For example, if asked "How much do you smoke?" a smoker who smokes 4 packs a day may purposely report smoking only 2 packs a day because they are embarrassed to admit the correct number. Or, the smoker may simply not answer the question, regarding it as a private matter. (These are examples of being *unwilling* to report a known answer.) But it is also possible that a smoker who smokes 4 packs a day may report smoking only 2 packs because they honestly believe they only smoke about 2 packs a day. (Unknowingly giving an incorrect answer is sometimes called self-deception; this illustrates being *unable* to give the desired answer).

The unwilling–unable distinction is like the difference between purposely hiding something from others and unconsciously hiding something from yourself. The Implicit Association Test makes it possible to penetrate both of these types of hiding. The IAT measures *implicit* attitudes and beliefs that people are either unwilling or unable to report.

(From the Project Implicit website. Retrieved June 14, 2007 from https://implicit.harvard.edu/implicit/demo/background/index.jsp)

- Students will evaluate messages about gender that they receive in print and broadcast media and in their everyday lives.
- Students will become more aware of tacit and explicit media messages.
- Students will be able to discuss bias in helpful and appropriate ways.
- Students will explore differences between immediately accessible mental constructs and beliefs.

CONNECTIONS TO STANDARDS

- *Language Arts Writing Standard 1:* Uses general skills and strategies of the writing process.
- *Language Arts Writing Standard 4:* Gathers and uses information for research purposes.
- *Technology Standard 1:* Knows the characteristics and uses of computer hardware and operating systems.
- *Technology Standard 2:* Knows the characteristics and uses of computer software programs.
- *Visual Arts Standard 4:* Understands the visual arts in relation to history and cultures.
- *World Language Standard 5:* Understands that different languages use different patterns to communicate and applies this knowledge to the target and native languages.

(Copyright 2007. Reprinted with permission from *Content Knowledge: A Compendium of Standards and Benchmarks for K-12 Education,* 4th ed. http://www.mcrel.org/standards-benchmarks/ All rights reserved.)

MATERIALS

- Television and VCR
- Excerpts from popular TV shows and print advertisements that demonstrate gender roles (many excellent print ads are available at http://www.genderads.com).
- Class computers with access to the Internet
- Implicit Association Tests (must be taken online at https://implicit.harvard.edu/implicit)

ACTIVITY

1. Start the class by writing the following sentences on the board:
   a. I allow my son/daughter to join the class field trip.
   b. S/he will participate in a study of attitudes.
   c. Mrs. Kellum will not join Mr. Waverly in the activity.
   d. *Ellos están contentos.* (Note: Use references in any other languages that you know or are spoken in your school.)

   Ask students to point out gender references in each phrase and make comments about the implications of each. For example:

   a. The male-related word *son* always seems to preceed the female word *daughter.*
   b. The pronoun can be split to represent both male and female; in this case, the female word is part of the male term.
   c. For many years (and still today), the titles revealed marital status for women, yet not for men. In this example, we know that *Mrs.* Kellum is married, but we do not know *Mr.* Waverly's marital status.
   d. In Spanish, when there is a mixed gender group of people, the male pronoun (in this case *ellos*) is always used. Even if there were one thousand women and only one man, the male pronoun must be used.

2. Have a discussion about gender as revealed in language with students. For students who speak languages other than English and/or for those who are studying a foreign language in school, have a discussion about gender references in different languages. Are there other grammatical rules that reveal gender biases?

3. Explain to students that they will be taking an online Implicit Association Test (IAT). This test will assess students' conscious and unconscious preferences and will measure hidden biases.

4. Before taking the test, have students answer the following question in their journal: Do you expect stereotypes to affect your performance on the test, or are you confident that social prejudices will not influence you?

5. Have students take the Gender-Career IAT by following these steps:

   a. Go to the Project Implication Website: http://implicit.harvard.edu.
   b. Click on "demonstration"
   c. Read the "Preliminary Information" and then click, "I wish to proceed" at the bottom of the page.
   d. Click on the "Gender-Career IAT" and proceed with the test.

   They will need approximately 5–10 minutes to take the test online.

6. After taking the test, have students answer the following questions in their journal: How do you feel about the results? Were they what you expected? Think about if and/or how you are exposed to negative stereotypes about gender. How often and where are these stereotypes reinforced in your everyday life?

7. Show students a variety of magazine advertisements and/or video clips that depict gender roles in the media. Have a class discussion about the roles presented.

8. Have students design a poster that highlights gender biases. Encourage students to think about using the poster as an educational tool with younger students.

ACTION PROJECT

For homework, ask students to watch at least one hour of television or a movie. Ask them to answer the following question in their journal: What gender roles are represented and/or reinforced in show/movie?

Have students create their own implicit association test for their classmates regarding gender images on TV or in the movies. Some possible questions on their survey:

- Name three strong men on TV.
- Name three caring men on TV.
- Name three caring women on TV.
- Name three strong women on TV.

The student should time interviewee's to see how long it takes to answer each question. After the tests, ask students to think about the following questions:

- Which questions were easier to answer?
- Which questions were harder to answer?
- What inferences might you draw from the tests?

REFLECTION

Did students' reactions to the advertisements surprise you in any way? What were the main stereotypes revealed through the ads in your class? How might reflection journals work in your own class? Are they a good way of encouraging students to think deeply about a topic or lesson? If so, in what ways? If not, why not? What are other ways that you might encourage students to reflect on a topic presented in class? Did you take the Gender-Career IAT? If so, did your results surprise you? Why or why not?

Lesson 23 adapted form Paula Davis' *Gender in the Media*. Used with permission.

CHAPTER 9

SEXUAL ORIENTATION

*Greatness meant strength. Strength meant masculinity. Masculinity meant
heterosexuality. Heterosexuality meant facade. Maintain facade for the world to see.
Cheat in the dark abyss of the soul.*

ARTHUR BELL (Canadian journalist, 1933–1984)

Some Background

It is perhaps still one of the only slurs left unpunished in schools today: "fag." Students
are taught about tolerance for difference and respect for diversity. They are exposed to
assemblies about bullying and they sign contracts promising not to discriminate or use
offensive language in school. And yet, take a stroll down any school hallway and you
are almost assured of hearing "faggot," "queer," or "gay" being used as a putdown from
one student to another.

Why are homophobic comments still a major part of schools? Teachers don't tolerate
the hurtful, provocative word "nigger" being tossed around on school grounds, but often
are reluctant to fight students over antigay comments. Is it possible that the lack of resis-
tance to homophobia in school has something to do with the perceived connection to sex?
Homosexuality comes under the heading of "sexual orientation" (as does even this chapter,
for lack of a better term), and many teachers are squeamish about addressing issues of
sexuality in their classroom. And yet homosexuality is as much about the actual sex act as
is heterosexuality—that is, not very much at all. Homosexuality is about families,
communities, love, and humanity—all fine topics for any school curriculum.

Educating our students to be tolerant, understanding and accepting of different lifestyles
is one of our goals in education. We must develop and integrate overt curricula that include all people in our schools. If the statistics are correct and 1 in every 10 people is gay,
then we are negligent in our duties if gay people—as parents, authors, scientists, heroes,
and community members—are excluded from our teaching.

Lesson Preparation for the Teacher

ONE TEACHER'S REFLECTION—BETRAYAL

*About 15 years ago, in my very classroom, the unthinkable happened. A young man, sitting in the
front row of my classroom on the opposite end of the room from the door, needed to leave the
classroom. When he returned, I, and I am sure he, heard the words "queer" and "faggot" from the
back of the room. He went back to his seat with the appearance of not hearing those painful words, and
I went on with my lesson, totally ignoring the pejoratives that came from the back of the room. Why did
I do that? I was afraid, as I had been for so many years. Sure, I was sort of out, but not totally. Sure, I
was the teacher and I could have helped that young man, but I chose not to. I often think of that boy*

and of that second-period class when I knew that I had betrayed both my student and myself for the zillionth time.

Over 25 years ago there was a student I had the feeling was gay. Of course I never suggested that some of his anxiety and attitude might stem from this possibility. He and I had a terrific student–teacher relationship. When he did not get a prize that he thought he deserved, he was hurt, so much so that his mom came to see me. He needed to excel all the time.

He needed to be more than what he was, both for himself and his family. On the last day of school, before he graduated, I told him that I saw much of myself in him and that if he ever needed to talk to an adult about his feelings, I was available. Many years later our paths crossed. He and I became friends. He shared with me his years of anxiety in school and that my thoughts about him were correct. I often thought that if I, who had a partner and a productive life, could have been a role model for him, he might not be taking antidepressant medication today, 25 years later. He might have just connected with his peers when he was in high school and not have gone through his life always scared of failure.

Recently a young man asked me how you get "gaydar." He wanted to know how to tell other gay people in the crowd. He wanted to find himself in the crowd. Even five years ago I would not have had that conversation with a student. Today, I, and my colleagues, encourage students to talk to me. One student just dropped in my office and asked me what it was like to come out. I told him. He left and says hello to me in the hall when he sees me. He knows there is an adult in the building he can go to when the roof crashes in.

Then there is me. As a teacher, there were so many missed opportunities to connect with students and demonstrate to them that their prejudices and fears were unfounded. During my first years as a teacher, I remained closeted and fearful. I was alone and probably not very open. This taught both the heterosexual and homosexual students the same lesson: good fags are quiet fags. Once a colleague of mine told me that a fellow faculty member didn't like me because I was not discreet about my sexuality. He thought I should have kept the fact that I had a partner to myself. He liked another homosexual in the building because that "homo" didn't talk about his private life. Thankfully, that kind of thinking doesn't affect me anymore.

Today, I refuse to return to the closet, a dark and fearful place. I encourage students to be honest about who they are, just as their parents and teachers all promote the truth. Yes, tell the truth, we all tell them. Well I agree, tell the truth in a loving way, but tell it. Free yourself and others from the closet.

TEACHER ACTION PROJECT: CONNECTING TO GLSEN

Visit the website of the Gay, Lesbian & Straight Education Network (http://www.glsen.org). This organization, designed for students and teachers, is aimed at education and establishing safe schools across the country. From the homepage, explore the "educators" section. Once in this area of the website, find one activity that you feel comfortable bringing to your school. For example, read about No Name-Calling Week and try to implement such an event in your district, school, or classroom. Or research and explore the possibility of establishing a Gay-Straight Alliance in your school. A less public alternative might be choosing a book from GLSEN's "BookLink" section (under "research") and forming a book club with other teachers to read and discuss the book. Whatever activity you choose, keep a journal that details your exploration. Include any obstacles you might face as well as your feelings in bringing this information to the school community.

References and Suggested Readings

Baker, J. M. (2002). *How homophobia hurts children: Nurturing diversity at home, at school, and in the community.* Binghampton, NY: Harrington Park.

Bauer, M. D. (1994). *Am I blue?: Coming out from the silence.* New York: Harper Collins.

Bennett, L. (1998). Teaching students to face their anti-gay prejudices. *Chronicle of Higher Education,* October 23, p. A76.

Casper, V., & Schultz, S. B. (1999). *Gay parents/straight schools: Building communication and trust.* New York: Teachers College Press.

D'Augelli, A. R., & Patterson, P. J. (Eds.). (2001). *Lesbian, gay, and bisexual identities and youth: Psychological perspectives.* Oxford, UK: Oxford University Press.

Harris, M. B. (Ed.). (1997). *School experiences of gay and lesbian youth: The invisible minority.* Binghampton, NY: Haworth.

Hogan, S., & Hudson, L. (1998). *Completely queer: The gay and lesbian encyclopedia.* New York: Henry Holt.

Huegel, K. (2003). *GLBTQ: The survival guide for queer and questioning teens.* Minneapolis, MN: Free Spirit.

Kissen, R. M. (1996). *The last closet: The real lives of lesbian and gay teachers.* Portsmouth, NH: Heinemann.

Kosciw, J. (Ed.). (2006). *The 2005 national school climate survey.* New York: Gay, Lesbian and Straight Education Network.

Lipkin, A. (1999). *Understanding homosexuality, changing schools: A text for teachers, counselors and administrators.* Boulder, CO: Westview.

Lipkin, A. (2003). *Beyond diversity day: A Q&A on gay and lesbian issues in schools.* Lanham, MD: Rowman & Littlefield.

Macgillivray, I. K. (2003). *Sexual orientation and school policy: A practical guide for teachers, administrators, and community activists.* Lanham, MD: Rowman & Littlefield.

Nardi, P. M., & Schneider, B. E. (Eds.). (1998). *Social perspectives in lesbian and gay studies: A reader.* New York: Routledge.

Pinar, W. (Ed.). (1998). *Queer theory in education.* Mahwah, NJ: Lawrence Erlbaum Associates.

Pollack, R., & Schwartz, C. (1995). *The journey out: A guide for and about lesbian, gay and bisexual teens.* New York: Viking.

Sears, J. T. (2005). *Gay, lesbian, and transgender issues in education: Programs, policies, and practice.* Binghampton, NY: Harrington Park.

Spurlin, W. (2000). *Lesbian and gay issues in the English classroom: Positions, pedagogies, and cultural politics.* Urbana, IL: National Council on the Teaching of English.

LESSON 25

FAMILIES OF ALL KINDS

GRADE LEVELS

Grades K–5

CONTENT AREAS ADDRESSED

Language Arts, Life Skills, Social Studies/History, Visual Arts

TOPIC

This lesson teaches children to be accepting of all families. Students will gain awareness and will understand that there are many different people, situations, and events outside of their own community. They will come to understand that their life and family is not necessarily the norm.

RATIONALE FOR USING THIS LESSON

This lesson uses one of two selected books to help students understand that each member of every school community should be valued and respected regardless of their sexual orientation or gender identity/expression at home. After the lesson, students will understand that such an atmosphere engenders a positive sense of self, which is the basis of educational achievement and personal growth at school and elsewhere.

You will want to think about what kinds of families exist for the children in your class. This could be new information for some children, while others have been exposed to a variety of families for a long time. Consider your audience, and in particular parents' reactions to introducing the selected book.

BACKGROUND INFORMATION: GAY PARENTS DO EXIST: LETTING THE RABBIT OUT OF THE HAT

The television show *Postcards From Buster* and its accompanying free lesson plans are used by social studies and language arts teachers in elementary and middle schools across the country. (1) In this animated half-hour show, Buster Baxter, a rabbit, travels with his father, who is piloting a fictional rock band on its North American concert tour. (2) Each episode finds Buster discovering new cultures and communities. He videotapes documentary "postcards" (featuring real people) that he sends to Arthur and his other (animated) friends back home. Classroom activities based on the show strengthen students' geography and language skills, in addition to building awareness and appreciation of the many cultures in America.

Earlier this year I experienced déjâ vu. PBS—the Public Broadcasting Service—decided not to distribute an episode in which Buster meets two children whose parents are lesbians. The same day, Secretary of Education Margaret Spelling sent PBS a letter demanding that the network not air it. "Many parents would not want their young children exposed to the lifestyles portrayed in the episode," she wrote. She also asked PBS to return federal funds used to make the episode, which was about maple sugaring in Vermont.

I flashed back to 1999, when a documentary I directed, *It's Elementary: Talking About Gay Issues in School*, was offered for broadcast through American Public Television. The film shows how and why schools are finding age-appropriate ways to address gay and lesbian issues in education: confronting rampant anti-gay name-calling, helping students to discuss gay-related topics as part of lessons on current events, and reading books that have characters with gay parents. When *It's Elementary* was scheduled to air on public television, PBS received more letters of protest than for any other program in its history. And what was PBS's response? Said Robert Conrad, then president of the Corporation for Public Broadcasting: "This sounds to me like a program that helps parents do a better job of parenting, and that is the kind of thing that public broadcasting has a right to do."

It made me wonder what kind of world Margaret Spelling and the executives at PBS are living in. It seems they think that there is one world where all the families and children live and somewhere over there, across the border, a separate world where all of those gay people live. Parents, they would argue (who must all be straight) should be the ones to decide if and when to let their children have a controlled peek at those inhabitants on the other side of that imaginary line. At this point in American history, such a position is not only ridiculous, it is insulting and highly irresponsible. The truth is that today, millions of children have a parent, uncle, aunt, cousin, sibling or grandparent who is gay. Thousands of dedicated teachers, school administrators and coaches are gays or lesbians. What kind of message are we sending to our youth when we say that their loved ones and trusted mentors aren't safe for children to meet on TV? That, in fact, is where the real potential danger lies. Think about the harm we are causing for all of those children when we say, "Sorry, your family has been censored today." Even if we keep Buster the bunny from visiting children whose parents are gay, we can't put the rabbit back in the hat. Gay people and gay issues are part of everyone's world now, including that of our children. Our only choice is whether we step up and give kids the skills and opportunities to treat everyone respectfully, or whether we try to perpetuate a false silence around the real lives of millions of Americans, a silence that is damaging to all young people.

(From Chasnoff, D. (2005). Gay parents do exist: letting the rabbit out of the hat. *Social Education, 69* (4), M2 (2). Reprinted by permission of the National Council for the Social Studies.)

GOALS/AIMS

- Students will understand that there are many different kinds of family units; there is no single "correct" definition of a family.
- Students will learn that antigay prejudice achieves nothing, fosters hatred, and does not promote a healthy school climate.

CONNECTIONS TO STANDARDS

- *History: Topic 1: Living and Working Together in Families and Communities, Now and Long Ago:* Understands family life now and in the past, and family life in various places long ago; understands the history of a local community and how communities in North America varied long ago.

- *Language Arts: Listening and Speaking Standard 8:* Uses listening and speaking strategies for different purposes.
- *Life Skills—Working with others: Standard 1:* Contributes to the overall effort of a group.
- *Life Skills—Working with others: Standard 4:* Displays effective interpersonal communication skills.
- *Life Skills—Working with others: Standard 5:* Demonstrates leadership skills.
- *Visual Arts Standard 1:* Understands and applies media, techniques, and processes related to the visual arts.

MATERIALS

- Chart paper
- Markers
- Paper for the students
- Crayons
- One of two books:
  1. *All Families Are Different*, by Sol Gordon.   The author looks at a variety of family structures, exploring issues such as adoption, multiracial families, foster homes, and same-sex families. The text places importance on children knowing they are loved by their family members, whoever they may be, while the illustrations depict a variety of family situations to stimulate awareness and acceptance.
  2. *Is Your Family Like Mine?*, by Lois Abramchik.   Armetha is a 5-year-old girl with two moms. She and her friends, all of whom come from different family constellations, discover that love is a common bond.

ACTIVITY

1. Introduce the topic of families. Possible script: "Today we are going to start our unit on families. I know that all of our families are extremely important to us. We all have different types of families, but the one thing in common is that we all really care about our families, no matter who they are. Let's start out by giving some examples of families and maybe a few definitions. Now remember, a family is made up of people you love. There is no right or wrong definition for a family. I am sure we will have a variety of families on this chart."

2. Call on students and listen to their answers, while charting them on paper labeled "the family." Possible script: "You all gave me such great answers. I was interested to hear about your families. We are going to start off this unit by reading a great book by [Sol Gordon/Lois Abramchik] that shows us the importance of families, and how each one is different, but love makes them all the same."

3. Read the book aloud. Afterward, encourage children to turn and talk to their partners about their reactions to the book, so as to get the "juices" flowing. Ask students the following questions:
   - What sorts of things did you notice in this book?
   - How is this book different from those that you usually read?
   - What was your favorite part?
   - What surprised you in this book?
   - Did you learn anything new?
   - Can you relate to any of the characters in this book?
   - Do you think that in this school/classroom, everyone's family looks the same (or is made up of similar people)?

- How would you feel if you were _____? (Fill in with characters from the book.)
- What are some things that families do? (i.e., have fun together, love each other, take care of one another. . . .)

4. After the discussion, have students draw not only their own family, but also some of the families they noticed in the book. Students can use any art materials they would like, such as markers, construction paper, or anything else that might help with their drawings. Students can also label and write a few sentences about their family.

5. After drawing, bring the children back to a circle, where they share their drawing with the class.

6. Conclude the lesson with a final discussion, emphasizing that there are many types of families and by highlighting some of the various family units that the students have drawn. Possible script: "In this book we saw that there were so many different kinds of families. However, we noticed that each family has something in common. We should keep in mind that not only in school, but in general, everyone's family is not the same. All families are important. Each family is unique and means a lot to each child. There is no such thing as a right or wrong family. We create our own families to include who we care most about."

7. Create a classroom gallery of the family portraits and have other classes, parents, and community members visit the gallery. Have students serve as docents and describe/narrate their artwork.

ACTION PROJECT

Have students adopt someone as a new member of their family. Explain to students that the person must be someone they can talk to about this "adoption." Ask them to think about the reasons why they would like to add this person to their family. For older students, have them write an "adoption proposal" for the person to read. Have the students contact their person and explain to them why they want them in their family. Ask students to report back their experiences in a "show and tell" format. They should bring a photo of their "adoptee" or possibly invite the person to visit class. Older students can write a journal entry about the experience.

REFLECTION

How did students react to the picturebooks? Did they have any questions that surprised you? If so, which ones? Are there any gay families in your school? If so, how are they treated by your colleagues? By the school administration? By other families? What supports (if any) are in place in your school to ensure the acceptance and inclusion of diverse families?

Lesson 25 adapted from Debra Chasnoff, "Gay Parents Do Exist: Letting the Rabbit out of the Hat," *Middle Level Learning 23* (May/June 2005): M2-M3. Used with permission.

LESSON 26

AM I BLUE?

Go to the Take Action! DVD to view a video of this lesson, "Am I Blue?," in action.

GRADE LEVELS

Grades 6–8

CONTENT AREAS ADDRESSED

Language Arts, Mathematics, Theater

TOPIC

Homophobia and sexual identity issues are addressed in a poignant and funny short story about a teenager who gets beaten up by a boy who suspects him of being gay. When his fairy godfather appears, the boy is treated to three wishes—one of which involves identifying anyone who is gay by a blue color.

RATIONALE FOR USING THIS LESSON

Middle school students are notorious for their relentless use of antigay and homophobic slurs among their peers. When pressed to explain why they use the term "gay" as a pejorative term, they often say that they are just joking, or that it doesn't mean "homosexual." By highlighting the negative effects of antigay talk, teachers can make students more aware of the way in which their language causes harm. Students will also come to understand that many people that they love and respect are gay and that everyone deserves respect and kindness regardless of their sexual orientation.

BACKGROUND INFORMATION: KEY FINDINGS OF THE 2005 NATIONAL SCHOOL CLIMATE SURVEY

The Gay, Lesbian and Straight Education Network, or GLSEN, conducts the only national survey to document the experiences of students who identify as lesbian, gay, bisexual and transgender (LGBT) in America's schools.

"The 2005 National School Climate Survey reveals that anti-LGBT bullying and harassment remain commonplace in America's schools," said GLSEN Founder and Executive Director Kevin Jennings. "On the positive side, it also makes clear that inclusive policies, supportive school staff and student clubs, like Gay-Straight Alliances, all relate to reduced harassment and higher achieving students."

The Scope of the Problem

- 75.4% of students heard derogatory remarks such as "faggot" or "dyke" frequently or often at school, and nearly 9 out of 10 (89.2%) reported hearing "that's so gay" or "you're so gay"—meaning stupid or worthless— frequently or often.

- Over a third (37.8%) of students experienced physical harassment at school on the basis of sexual orientation and more than a quarter (26.1%) on the basis of their gender expression. Nearly one-fifth (17.6%) of students had been physically assaulted because of their sexual orientation and over a tenth (11.8%) because of their gender expression.

Academic Engagement, Aspirations and Achievement

- LGBT students were five times more likely to report having skipped school in the last month because of safety concerns than the general population of students.
- LGBT students who experience more frequent physical harassment were more likely to report they did not plan to go to college. Overall, LGBT students were twice as likely as the general population of students to report they were not planning to pursue any postsecondary education.
- The average GPA for LGBT students who were frequently physically harassed was half a grade lower than that of LGBT students experiencing less harassment (2.6 versus 3.1).

Positive Interventions and Support

- The presence of supportive staff contributed to a range of positive indicators including greater sense of safety, fewer reports of missing days of school, and a higher incidence of planning to attend college.
- Students in schools with a GSA were less likely to feel unsafe, less likely to miss school, and more likely to feel like they belonged at their school than students in schools with no such clubs.
- Having a comprehensive policy was related to a lower incidence of hearing homophobic remarks and to lower rates of verbal harassment. Students at schools with inclusive policies also reported higher rates of intervention by school staff when homophobic remarks were made.

(From Kosciw, J. G., & Diaz, E. M. (2006). *The 2005 National School Climate Survey: The experiences of lesbian, gay, bisexual and transgender youth in our nation's schools.* Retrieved June 14, 2007 from http://www.glsen.org/cgi-bin/iowa/all/library/record/1927.html. Reprinted by permission of GLSEN).

GOALS/AIMS

- Students will be able to understand the effects of name-calling, antigay language, and homophobic comments.
- Students will be able to understand the difficulties and pain of having to hide one's identity in school.
- Students will be able to analyze a story and identify its main literary elements.
- Students will be able to develop, write, and perform a play that highlights some of the points gleaned from the short story.

CONNECTIONS TO STANDARDS

- *Language Arts: Writing Standard 1:* Uses the general skills and strategies of the writing process.
- *Language Arts: Writing Standard 2:* Uses the stylistic and rhetorical aspects of writing.
- *Language Arts: Reading Standard 5:* Uses the skills and strategies of the reading process.
- *Language Arts: Reading Standard 6:* Uses reading skills and strategies to understand a variety of literary texts.

- *Mathematics Standard 6:* Understands and applies basic and advanced concepts of statistics and data analysis.
- *Mathematics Standard 8:* Understands and applies basic and advanced properties of functions and algebra. (Understands how graphs can represent patterns.)
- *Theater Standard 1:* Demonstrates competence in writing scripts.
- *Theater Standard 2:* Uses acting skills.
- *Theater Standard 3:* Designs and produces informal and formal productions.

MATERIALS

- A copy of the story "Am I Blue?" by Bruce Coville (from M. D. Bauer (Ed.), *Am I Blue?: Coming Out of the Silence*, New York: Harper Collins, 1994).

ACTIVITY

1. *Discrimination free write.* Have students write about an experience, a feeling, or anything relating to the word/term *discrimination.* Students can use the following questions as a prompt:
   - What does it mean to be discriminated against?
   - Have you ever been discriminated against because of your race, religion, gender, age, or other characteristic? Explain.
   - Have you ever heard someone else be discriminated against because of her/his race, religion, gender, age, or other characteristic? Explain.
   - Have you ever read about or seen in a movie someone discriminated against because of her/his race, religion, gender, age, or other characteristic? Explain.

2. Distribute copies of "Am I Blue?" to students. Read the text out loud as students read along. Encourage them to underline, highlight, or otherwise annotate the text as they read. They can highlight any portion (i.e., something that surprises them, confuses them, makes them sad, makes them smile, etc.).

3. At page 13, have students do a double-entry journal. Have them write any questions, comments, or opinions in the margins of the story.

4. Stop reading at page 15 at the "three wishes" part of the story. At this point, have students predict how the story will end.

5. Have students exchange their predictions with a classmate. Encourage partners to agree or disagree with each other's predictions and explain why. Have several students write their predictions on the board to discuss with the class.

6. Ask the following questions:
   - What do you think so far about the text?
   - What do you think about Vince? Melvin?
   - What is your opinion about how Melvin dies?
   - What is your opinion of what Butch did to Vince?

   Have students share their thoughts/responses.

7. Share information about Matthew Shepard and discuss. Here is a brief narrative:

   One night in a bar in Laramie, Wisconsin, a young college student, Matthew Shepard, met two men and reportedly asked one of them for a ride home. On that fatal ride home, the two men brutally beat Shepard, fracturing his head so severely that he suffered brain stem damage as a result. After the beating, he was tied to a fence in a very isolated, remote area and left there to die. When he was finally discovered and brought to the hospital, the wounds he suffered to his head, face, and neck were too severe to operate. He died several days later. The two men were later arrested. A bloody gun and the victim's shoes and wallet were found in one of the men's car. Both men were arrested and charged with murder and are now serving time in jail for their horrible crime.

8. Finish reading the story aloud. Ask the students a concluding question: "Butch beats up Vince in the beginning of the story because he thinks Vince is gay. At the end of the story, we find out that Butch, himself, is gay. Why, then, would he beat up Vince?" Discuss students' responses (Figure 9.1).

9. Share the following definitions with students:

   Heterosexual: A romantic attraction between two individuals of opposite genders.

   Homosexual (Gay/Lesbian): A romantic attraction between two individuals of the same gender.

10. Talk about the expression "That's so gay!" Ask students if they have ever heard that expression in the halls, at home, on the playground, etc. Unpack its meaning by asking students what the expression means to them.

11. Do a "good/bad" T chart (Figure 9.2), with students brainstorming synonyms for good (i.e., *awesome, amazing, fantastic*, etc.) and bad (i.e., *terrible, awful, nasty*, etc.) Ask students where the word *gay* fits into the chart.

Figure 9.1   Sample student responses.

Why, then, would he beat up Vince?

—B/c he is covering up the fact that he is also gay.

—B/c Butch is not scared of gays but he was in denial and trying to convince himself that he was not gay.

—B/c he wanted to prove to himself and his friends that he wasn't gay.

—By being mean to gays, he made it look like he wasn't gay.

End of Story Questions

Figure 9.2   Sample student responses.

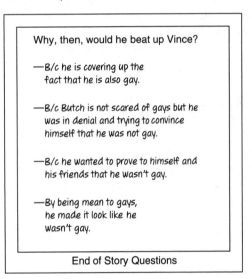

THAT'S SO GAY!

What does that mean?

If you want to say something is good, you say, "That's so ___great___ ."	If you want to say something is bad, you say, "That's so ___lame___ ."
awesome	stupid
hot	annoying
cool	ternby
fantastic	
fly	

Good/Bad Chart

Ask students to think about what lessons or advice we might take away from these examples.

12. Direct students' attention back to the story. Ask them the following questions:

- What observations does Vince make when he is able to "see" blue?
- How might different people feel when they hear the expression "That's so gay!"?

13. *Conclusion* have students brainstorm ways in which to change the use of the word in school. Some possible prompts:

- Think Before You Speak: Before you say something to someone, think about how your words will be received by the other person.
- Speak Thoughtfully: Be sure to use your mind and your heart when you are speaking.
- Think, So You Know: Take a few minutes every once in a while to think about your feelings and opinions on certain issues. Educate yourself so that you will be confident in your knowledge when you are called on to talk about a topic.

ACTION PROJECT

Have students create a dramatic version of the story "Am I Blue," such as a short movie or a play. Encourage students to take their version "on the road" and show or perform it for the rest of your school, and possibly for other schools in your district or community. Have them also design a contract that audience members can sign after seeing the movie/play that encourages them to promise to not use hurtful or disrespectful language in school, in the workplace, or in the community. Collect the contracts and send them to the principal of your school. Encourage the principal to declare a "no name-calling day" in your school.

REFLECTION

How did students react to the story "Am I Blue"? Were you surprised by any of their comments? Do you know any gay students or teachers in the school? Are they treated any differently by classmates and/or colleagues? Do they hide their identity, or are they "out"? How is homosexuality regarded in your school's culture?

Lesson 26 adapted from Michele DeVirgilio's *Am I Blue?* Used with permission.

LESSON 27

LEARNING SOCIAL ROLES

GRADE LEVELS

Grades 9–12

CONTENT AREAS ADDRESSED

Language Arts, Life Skills, Music, Technology

TOPIC

This activity continues self-reflective processes as participants write and share short pieces about how their sexual identities were affected through childhood messages—and lyrics to popular music—about what it means to be straight or gay. This activity can be used to introduce a discussion on sexual orientation, setting the groundwork for maintaining a focus on talking about issues from one's own personal experience.

RATIONALE FOR USING THIS LESSON

Because most all students listen to popular music, they can relate to a lesson that involves them in dissecting lyrics and analyzing them for messages being sent regarding sexual orientation. Students can come to be more critical of the media portrayal of acceptable behavior as it relates to being gay or straight.

BACKGROUND INFORMATION: BEENIE MAN'S HOMOPHOBIC LYRICS

London, 16 August 2004—EMI and Virgin Records are being condemned for signing and promoting Jamaican reggae star, Beenie Man, following his call for the "execution" of gay people.

The condemnation comes the day EMI/Virgin Records releases Beenie Man's new album, *Back to Basics* (today, 16 August 2004).

Peter Tatchell of the gay human rights group OutRage!, has written to the President of Virgin Records and the Chief Executive of parent company EMI, Tony Wadsworth. . . . .

He points out that four of Beenie Man's past songs urge listeners to "shoot" and "hang" people he abuses as "queers," "faggots" and "bum-fuckers". . . . .

Mr. Tatchell's letters to EMI and Virgin state:

"Despite his so-called apology, these incitement to murder songs are still selling and Beenie Man is still profiteering from his murder music."

"Inciting murder is a criminal offence: Free speech does not include the right to encourage the criminal act of murder."

The *OutRage!* letter calls on Virgin Records to "either cancel Beenie Man's contract or agree to:

1. Arrange the public broadcast of a video and audio statement by Beenie Man apologising explicitly to the lesbian and gay community for inciting homophobic violence, and

2. Either buy up the rights and existing copies of his songs inciting homophobic murder, or donate all royalties from these songs to a charity that helps the victims of queer-bashing violence."

(From Tatchell, P. (2004). BEENIE MAN'S HOMOPHOBIC LYRICS *OutRage!* writes to EMI and Virgin Records. Retrieved June 14, 2007 from http://www.ilga.org/print.asp?FileCategory=54&FileID=294&ZoneID=5&)

GOALS/AIMS

- Students will be able to write a personal narrative regarding the influences they have experienced with regard to sexual orientation.
- Students will be able to be critical of popular music lyrics and analyze them for messages about sexual orientation.
- Students will be able to write a business letter in protest or in favor of the song lyrics of an artist of their choice.

CONNECTIONS TO STANDARDS

- *Language Arts: Writing Standard 1:* Uses the general skills and strategies of the writing process.
- *Language Arts: Writing Standard 2:* Uses the stylistic and rhetorical aspects of writing.
- *Language Arts: Reading Standard 1:* Uses the skills and strategies of the reading process.
- *Language Arts: Reading Standard 2:* Uses reading skills and strategies to understand a variety of informational texts.
- *Life Skills—Working with others: Standard 1:* Contributes to the overall effort of a group.
- *Life Skills—Working with others: Standard 4:* Displays effective interpersonal communication skills.
- *Life Skills—Working with others: Standard 5:* Demonstrates leadership skills.
- *Music Standard 6:* Knows and applies appropriate criteria to music and music performances.
- *Music Standard 7:* Understands the relationship between music and history and culture.
- *Technology Standard 6:* Understands the nature and uses of different forms of technology.

(Copyright 2007. Reprinted with permission from *Content Knowledge: A Compendium of Standards and Benchmarks for K-12 Education,* 4th ed. http://www.mcrel.org/standards-benchmarks/ All rights reserved.)

MATERIALS

- Access to computers with the Internet or samples of music with lyrics for analysis.
- CD player, MP3 player, or cassette player.

ACTIVITY

1. Ask students to write a short (1–2 page) reflective piece on their childhood memories and experiences that helped shape their sexual identities. (You may need to

assign this during a meeting or two prior to when you want to facilitate a conversation about it.) Ask them to address what messages they received as children about love, marriage, and romance. Also, ask them to discuss who sent those messages (parents, teachers, coaches, other students, etc.). Be clear that this is not to be an academic piece, but a reflective effort regarding their own experiences. (Note: Because some individuals will include very personal information, some may be hesitant to read their work, even in the small groups. It is sometimes effective in such situations for facilitators to share their own reflections first. Consider sharing yours when you give this assignment. If you make yourself vulnerable, others will be more comfortable doing the same.)

2. To ensure that everybody has an opportunity to share their story, break into diverse small groups. Give students the option either to read their pieces or to share their pieces and reflections from memory. Ask for volunteers to share their stories.

3. After everyone has shared their stories, discuss some of the following questions with the class:

   • Have you ever systematically considered how you developed your sexual identity?
   • How is your sexual identity still informed or affected by your experiences growing up?
   • What messages do you send to others regarding what it means to date, get married, or start a family?
   • How did (has) your schooling play into your understanding of what it meant (means) to be straight or gay?
   • Have you ever been ridiculed for doing or saying something that others didn't consider "masculine" or "feminine"? How did that make you feel? How did you react?
   • Have you ever ridiculed someone else for doing something you didn't consider "masculine" or "feminine"?
   • What messages are sent through popular music about sexuality?

4. Have students work in small groups to collect popular music with examples of messages regarding sexual orientation. Do any of their favorite songs contain antigay or homophobic lyrics? Have students work in small teams to collect examples of messages regarding sexual orientation in music. Some examples of popular songs about homosexuality:

Rated "G"

   • "Come to My Window" by Melissa Etheridge
   • "Coming Clean" by Green Day
   • "Outside" by George Michael
   • "The Killing of Georgie (Part 1 and 2)" by Rod Stewart

Rated "PG" (some language and/or sexual references)

   • "All The Girls Love Alice" by Elton John
   • "Handsome Devil" by The Smiths
   • "Lola" by The Kinks
   • "My Lovely Man" by Red Hot Chili Peppers
   • "Sexuality" by Billy Bragg

Ask each group to report their findings back to the class. (Note: Many of these lyrics are ambiguous or have more than one meaning. Encourage students to articulate their own interpretations of the songs in their oral presentations.)

ACTION PROJECT

Have the class develop a list of songs that contain antigay or homophobic lyrics. Ask students to design a website that lists these songs as a means of educating the public about the issue. Encourage students to include essays or their own reactions to the homophobic lyrics as part of the website. Have students share their lists and reactions with the younger students in the school and community.

REFLECTION

Can any messages sent in the lyrics of your favorite songs be considered antigay or homophobic? If so, which ones? Do the lyrics interfere with your enjoyment of the music? If so, why? If not, why not? Are there any musical genres in which homophobia is either accepted or promoted?

Lesson 27 adapted from Paul C. Gorski's, *Learning Social Roles*. Used with permission.

■ NAME INDEX

◼ SUBJECT INDEX